CW00847331

Gospel Glimpses fron

by Emma Bunday

Gospel Glimpses from the Heart

copyright 2011 Emma Bunday

All rights reserved

ISBN: 978-0-557-58725-4

Illustration copyright 2011 Johanna Wilbraham
Used with kind permission

Dedicated to my beloved, encouraging husband,
Jonathan

Gospel Glimpses from the Heart

Contents

Introduction

1. The Birth   1
   Poem – The Birth   4

2. Dorcas   6
   Poem – Water into Wine   13

3. Peter - Whilst you were sleeping   14
   Poem – Water at the Well   19

4. From Despair to Deliverance   20
   Poem –Jesus came   27

5. Encounter with Jesus Part 1: Lydia   28
   Poem – Peter's Song   38

6. Martha Part 1: Martha   41
   Poem – Senses   59

7. John: The Lord's Prayer   62
   Poem – Quiet time?   67

8. Encounter with Jesus Part 2: Miriam   68
   Poem – Bread   91

9. The Tenth Leper   92
   Poem – Forgiven   110

10. Zacchaeus   112
    Poem – Imagine   132

11. Martha Part 2: Lazarus   133
     Poem – Freedom Fighter   150

12. Martha Part 3: Mary   152
     Poem – Worship   171

13. Lazarus: Bethany   172
     Poem – Fear   179

14. Andrew: The Last Supper   181
     Poem – Sit with Me   185

15. Jesus at Prayer   186
     Poem – Gethsemane   191

16.   Encounter with Jesus Part 3: The Thief   192
     Poem – Love is Bleeding   203

17. The Crucifixion   204
     Poem – The Passion   209

18. Dinah: On the beach   210
     Poem – Fish   226

     References   229

     About the Author   231

Introduction

The stories in this book are based on stories in the Bible.
I have, however, used my imagination to tell them from different and unfamiliar points of view.

The stories do not need to be read in order, although it might be helpful to do so when it comes to the ones written with 'parts' (i.e. 'Martha' and 'Encounters with Jesus').

I do suggest, though, that the reader does not read too many stories in one go.

Perhaps read each one slowly, then put the book down after reading a story, meditation or poem. Take time to reflect upon it and even 'imagine yourself' into the story you have just read.

I hope and pray that you will be blessed through these thoughts.

The Birth

It was the strangest day in heaven. Heaven generally had an unchanging feel about it. It throbbed with life. Harmonies and songs always filled the air. Joy and love were all around. There were changes, of course - daily more Saints arrived after living their earth lives, but the basic feel of heaven - vibrant and alive - was usually the same. The times when heaven's foundations were shaken were few enough to be numbered on the fingers of one hand.

But this day was different.

The angels themselves were surprised.

As Digital walked down the golden street, towards the crystal clear river, he was acutely aware that something foundational had shifted. It was more than the strange hush – it was almost in the air he breathed.

He was being drawn to the centre of all things almost without realising it.

He grew nearer. As usual there was a shining throng of angels around the throne but, for once, they were silent.

Over the wings, he could see what lay ahead – the emerald rainbow pulsing with life. Growing closer, easing himself through the winged beings, he glimpsed the throne itself.

It was empty.

He caught his breath. Now he understood the silence. He knew what this meant.

The whole of heaven had waited for this moment – now were the prophecies fulfilled.

Digital whispered into Joyful's ear, "When?" he asked.
"Just now," came the reply.

More angels were gathering by the moment, drawn by the same sense that something of the Glory was missing. As they, too, saw the empty throne, they understood what had happened. Myriads more arrived.

Some were missing, of course. Some had been despatched to earth to herald in the good news. Part of heaven was visiting earth, and it would never be the same again.

Still more gathered around the empty throne. Thousands upon thousands. Ten times ten thousand were silent. Their hearing was strained, tuned in to planet earth. Waiting...waiting...waiting...

Suddenly a noise was heard. A mere whimper, but every last angel heard it – it was what they had been listening for. It was a weak, helpless cry rising from a stable in Bethlehem.

A collective sigh sounded in heaven as the angels released the breaths they were barely aware they had been holding.

God – The Mighty Creator – was of course still with them. Yet a part of Him inexplicably was not there. His voice rang out,

"Now is the Glory of God come to man."

And for thirty three years the throne remained vacant, though the Father stood by it, still ruling, still reigning. For thirty three years, part of heaven was missing.

And Jesus walked the earth.

▪▪▪

Meditation

Consider how Jesus relinquished his heavenly position, his divine privileges, his very equality with God in order to come to earth in human form.

He did not relinquish such things reluctantly, but came willingly and joyfully, intent on redeeming his children and revealing the person and love of the Father to them.

Spend some time considering this, and let thankfulness and worship rise up from your heart towards him.

Poem - The Birth

A great and wondrous sign appeared in heaven.
Was it a moving star, drawing all who followed to the stable?
Or could it have been a woman?

Mary
Innocent, trusting virgin.
Handmaiden dressed in blue.
Tiredly heavy with child,
riding a donkey.
Humbly obedient - is this how you see her?

Or is it Mary -
God's hand-picked mother
Clothed with the sun
Moon under her feet
Radiant and shining
with her crown of twelve stars?

Do you think the birth was a peaceful affair
resulting in the little bundle of swaddling robes -
the donkey, the ox, the sheep - all standing by, doe-eyed
waiting by the manger, by the baby meek and mild?

Or do you hear Mary's screams of pain
as she sees the red dragon,
huge and menacing,
poised before her?
Sweeping stars to the earth with his tail.
Seven red heads waiting,
breathing fire, drooling
waiting to devour the child when it is born.

Are you watching the shepherds watching?
Darkness split by light as the angel appears.
'Glory to God' rings out across the silent mountains
The stars all twinkling with joy.

Look higher, look up, see heaven at war
See fire and smoke and grappling above.
The red dragon.
His ten horns waving and flailing and dodging and gouging
fighting the angels.
Flashes of brightness,
mighty Michael commanding the angels.
Rallying and battling in the name of The Lord
Dazzling bursts of grim pure whiteness.

Heaven's righteous strength victorious
defeats the dragon deceiver.
The crowns tumble from his seven heads
as he comes crashing down
with his paltry sidekicks
stripped of authority
he crashes to earth
to wreak the havoc he can there.

Mary fleeing to a place prepared by God
running into His cave.

The dragon fuming - he knows his time is short now.

The babe safe - waiting to grow to be a king.

The angels triumphant - exalting
Heaven crying with one accord:

"Now has come salvation and power and the kingdom of our
God."

Dorcas

The fishermen were, by degrees, puzzled, excited, doubtful, hopeful and confused. Just who was this man? The audacious things he had said in Nazareth - plain as you like – in the synagogue of all places! Quoting Isaiah 61 and claiming it to be fulfilled, right here, right now...could he have really meant that it was fulfilled in him? No wonder the Nazarenes had been furious. No wonder word of it had spread ahead of him. It was bordering on blasphemy.

Simon had not been there. He lived in Capernaum. But then Jesus had come to Capernaum itself. Again, he came to the synagogue and taught with incredible authority. All of Simon's friends were talking about it. John, especially, was won over. Gripped with a feverish excitement, he told Simon all about it, tripping over his words with excitement,

"Simon - it was amazing. I've never heard truth spoken so clearly. As he spoke you thought, 'of course...' everything made perfect sense... it was simple. And then," John paused, remembering, and his voice intensified even though he grew quieter. "A stranger called out. A crazy man. He called Jesus the 'Holy One of God'. He seemed to know that Jesus was from Nazareth - maybe he had followed him from there. But he shouted this 'Holy One of God' right across the synagogue. He was out of control. Like demons possessed him. After his shout, everyone watched Jesus to see what he would do." Again, John paused.

"Well?" Simon was drawn into the story. John was normally a quiet, thoughtful lad. But today he was tripping over his words with excitement. That in itself caught Simon's attention. "So what did he do?"

John resumed the story.

"We were all wondering - having claimed Isaiah 61 was about him, what could he do or say? Would he say he was from God? Was he Holy? It was the perfect moment for him to state who he was, if he was indeed from God. But Simon - I don't think he thought of himself. He looked across at the crazy man not with excitement or challenge, or even anger. I stood nearby and saw his piercing look, as if he looked into the man's soul and saw a man tormented and imprisoned. There was a flash of compassion in his eyes, and then they hardened as with great authority he said - and he didn't shout - he just spoke - 'Come out of him'. Immediately the man fell down. He fell heavily, as if he'd been thrown and yet, when he rose, he was not hurt, and he was...well, different. His face looked different. The crazed look had gone. He was puzzled and grateful. Truly, I think a demon had left him - all the people said so. So - who is this Jesus?"

Simon sighed. He was annoyed that he had not been there. But there was too much to do. It being the Sabbath there had been no fishing last night - though that didn't make much difference with the little he had been bringing home lately. Where were the fish this season? But Dorcas, his mother-in-law, had complained just yesterday morning that she felt 'strange', and then the fever had hit her. Oh, that his wife were still alive to help care for her - but it was all down to Simon. He was worried. And he was scared. These fevers hit quickly and they hit hard - they burned a person up. They could kill someone of Dorcas's age.

And here was John, raving about some holy man. Yet he wished he had met this Jesus. Something stirred deep in his heart when he heard about the man. But he had missed it now. Jesus was just visiting, wasn't he? Soon he would go back to Nazareth, or on to the next place. Just as Simon missed the fish, he had missed the man too. He glanced outside. The sun was high. He should check on Dorcas – try and get some food or drink down her - though she had little appetite.

The door to the house was open and, as Simon was looking at it, thinking of all that needed doing, the light was suddenly blocked. By a man. Simon thought for a second that he recognised him. There was a jolt in his heart. Then he realised it was a stranger. He sensed John had stiffened beside him, and he glanced at the young man. John was transfixed. His face was red - was he blushing? And then John let out the word, delighted shock in his voice "Jesus!"

Now it was Simon's turn to stare. He was too surprised to say a word. A boyish grin spread across the visitor's face and, without waiting to be invited, he just walked in. Perhaps John's welcoming cry was enough to draw him in.

Simon pulled himself together, feeling ill-at-ease but strangely excited. "Jesus! John here was just telling me about you. In the synagogue. I wasn't there. My mother-in-law can't be left; she's unwell. I should warn you - there is fever in the house. I don't know if the priests would deem her clean or not. And it is the Sabbath." He was babbling - he didn't seem to be able to stop himself. "But you are welcome. I have no meal prepared but there is bread. Stay a while. If you want, that is…"

Quickly he rose, and cleared a space for Jesus to sit. Perhaps now he could find out for himself who this Jesus was – clearly John thought he was something special. He could hardly believe his luck – a private audience with the man who was the talk of the town.

Jesus stood still, watching the thoughts play across Simon's face. Gently, he asked, "Where is your mother-in-law?"

It took a moment for the question to register. Confused, Simon pointed. There was another room, off to the side. Hardly a room, really. Just an alcove, with no doorway. Just apart enough from the main room to allow a bit of privacy.

8

Simon spoke with urgency, "She really isn't well. Be careful..."

His voice tailed off as Jesus made his way there. Simon made as if to get up, and then sank back down again. He was confused and slightly panicked – what if Jesus went down with fever? What if Dorcas was unclean? She was a woman – what did Jesus want with a sick woman? What could possibly interest him? Bewildered, he looked to John for direction, but John's eyes were following Jesus. Jesus knelt down. They could only see his back as he crouched down to speak with Dorcas.

She was indeed full of fever. She was trying to sleep, but her sleep was disturbed. Her throat was dry and swollen, her head ached and a sheen of sweat was on her face. Her mind was lost in an aching dry fog. She was so tired. At times during the day she had been aware of Simon putting a cup of water to her mouth – but she pushed him away. It hurt to swallow. It helped when he wiped her face with a cold, wet cloth, but the feeling didn't last. Even when she had wakeful moments, she kept her eyes shut – the light hurt them. In her semi-conscious state, she fretted. She was aware that Simon was up in the night for her. How could he fish if he was tending to her night and day? She had felt useless ever since her daughter had died, but now she was worse than useless – she was a burden.

Somewhere in the fog she became aware of something. Someone? She sensed a still presence nearby. Simon? Her muddled mind tried to work it out. But Simon fidgeted and fussed, unlike this presence beside her. She felt a gentle touch on her forehead; her hand was held in a cool, strong grip.

A low voice spoke. A commanding voice. A voice with authority. She heard some of the words and her eyes suddenly opened wide. She caught a sort of white flash of brightness, very different to the hot golden streaks of sunlight that penetrated this part of

9

the room in the afternoon. Yet this brightness did not hurt her eyes. Again his hand passed over her forehead, and it was as if he was just brushing away the fog in her mind. She took a deep breath, and found it no longer hurt to breath. She swallowed, and found no pain in that either. With the hand the man was not holding, she reached for the nearby cup and took a draught. The water was strangely cool and refreshing. The fever had gone. Completely. He was pulling on her hand and she sat up. She should feel sticky or sweaty, but she just felt cool and refreshed. The wobbly feeling in her legs – the ache in them, and in her back – these things had just vanished. Slowly she put it all together in her mind whilst he waited patiently beside her, still holding her hand firmly. Now she looked into the warm brown eyes that regarded her with a kind interest. 'Who are you?' her mind asked, but she spoke no word, just gazed in wonder at him.

"Come," he urged, standing up. He was still holding her hand, so she rose with him. He didn't seem to care that she was not attired properly. And what was a man doing in her sleeping area, for goodness sake? And come to think of it - wasn't it the Sabbath too! What was Simon thinking - to let a man see her in this condition?

She reached out for a shawl and flung it around her shoulders. The man said nothing as he pulled her into the main room, though she had the sudden impression that he was amused. He had his arm loosely around her, and suddenly she felt more loved and wanted than she had felt for years. A lump sprang to her throat.

Her son was sitting near the fire, talking in a low voice with young John.

Simon glanced up, and now he moved. He leapt to his feet, shocked. "Mother!!" he cried, rushing to her side and pushing Jesus out of the way. "You should not be up - you need rest..." His voice died away as he felt the strength in her arms pushing him away. She held him at arms length and he looked closely at her.

"You're feeling better," he declared slowly. "The fever's gone. You are well..." There was wonder in his voice, and slowly he turned round to stare at Jesus. The man looked a little weary now, he realised, but still a smile played around his lips. "Jesus?" Simon whispered. "How did that happen? Praise be to the Lord, but... who are you?"

Now Jesus sank to the floor, sitting closely to John. John reached for a nearby flagon of wine and poured some into a cup. Jesus gestured for Simon to sit, and took the cup from John. He replied, "I, Simon, am a very hungry man."

Dorcas let out a chuckle. Her heart felt strangely free. She spoke, looking directly at Jesus, with unspoken gratitude in her eyes. "You, Jesus, are a man about to enjoy a culinary feast..."

And she set to it. Producing one of many meals that she would prepare for the men over the next few years. But it was the best of them.

Jesus grew, from that day, in stature and fame. He became renowned throughout the region and even as far away as Jerusalem. Word of his spectacular miracles spread. He turned water into wine, healed cripples, walked on water, calmed storms, even raised the dead.

But for Dorcas, the most wondrous miracle was the day he took the fever away from a useless old fisherman's mother. It was also the day she ceased to think of herself like that.

For Jesus had taken her hand, and whispered into the depths of her being - "You are worth it. It is for such as you that I have come."

11

Meditation

Do you ever feel like a burden? That you have nothing to give? That you are useless?

Imagine yourself lying on that bed, as Simon Peter's mother-in-law was – weak and helpless. Imagine Jesus approaching. Sense him kneel by your side. Imagine that it is your brow he strokes, your hand he touches. Imagine him whispering into your ear. They would be words of love and healing. What is he saying to you? Allow his healing words to penetrate until you can see him clearly.

Imagine standing up with him. Dorcas' grateful response was to simply cook a meal for him. What is yours? Jesus is no longer with us in person but he says 'whatever you do for the least of these, you do for me.' We can still cook him meals, help him, love him, by our actions towards others.

Poem - Water into Wine

Water.
You took water.
Filled the jars with it.
Transformed to wine
and the best of wine to be had was theirs.

Life.
You took life.
Filled yourself with it.
Transformed to death
and more life than we ever dreamt of was ours.

Me.
You take me.
Fill yourself with me.
Transforming me
and a kind of love beyond imagining is mine.

Help me
To drink it
To live it
To know it.

Peter - Whilst you were sleeping

There was an enemy.

More subtle than the religious leaders though, like them, he craved control. Once a worshipper of the one true God, now he desired worship for himself.

Always he lurked. More dangerous than men, for this was a Spiritual being who regarded Jesus with utter hatred.

He took the form of a dragon to fight against the incarnation itself. But his attack was thwarted.

He watched and waited. Always on the lookout for a chance to destroy the Son of God who called himself the Son of Man. Obsessed with the idea of murdering God. Here was evil personified.

He had confronted Jesus face to face by now, of course. The defeat still stung. He had tried to twist the Word of God to his own ends, but that tactic would not prevail against he who was the Word of God. Jesus emerged from the desert, as full of the Spirit as when he had entered it. So his enemy waited. He would have to find a moment when Jesus was off his guard.

■■

The early days of simply listening to Jesus and being with him were at an end. We were more than ready for excitement when he laid out his plans to travel before us. That we were invited to go with such a man! To be in his inner circle of friends!

It made fishing seem ordinary, and I was the one who most loved fishing. I loved learning to judge the wind and the waves, discerning the whereabouts of the fickle shoals in any given weather or season. I loved the feel of the boat under my feet. I was steady when it bucked and rolled. I loved the still darkness of the night, the glowing phosphorescence of the water, the reflection of the moon in its depths. I loved working with my brothers, ringing out the orders but also working beside them. The sheer delight of nets that heaved with fish. The triumphant victory of landing a huge catch outweighed the drearier nights when the fish hid from us.

But those days lay in the past now. When Jesus urged us to 'come and follow', a different excitement made me obey. Fishing was my passion and my life, but it did not bring life to my innermost being in the way that simply a word or a touch from this man could.

Some days were spent on the road between villages, others in the villages themselves where crowds were beginning to gather when they saw Jesus. On the Sabbath we would visit whichever synagogue was the nearest. There were debates with the religious leaders, and teaching that cut into your very heart. And the healings! The miracles! What was a heaving net of fish compared to seeing a man's sight restored, or – heaven be praised – the sight of a boy stepping out of his coffin!

The heady days of miracles and the days of travelling and preaching, together with the early morning walks that Jesus would often take, took a toll. Many evenings we would look to him to answer a point we were debating, only to find he had dropped off to sleep, right where he sat.

Sometimes when visiting the villages and towns around the Sea of Galilee, we would travel by boat. I loved those times, for the call of the sea still ran through my blood, though not as strongly as the call of the son.

It was on such a journey that the mother and father of all storms hit us. It was one of those times when Jesus was weary. Perhaps too weary to walk, so we took a boat and set out. Before long, Jesus announced he would take a nap, and then fell into a deep sleep of exhaustion.

The Sea of Galilee can be unpredictable, but I know this large body of water. I grew up here. I was taken on a boat before I could walk. I would watch the skies as I mended the nets as a child. I knew their moods. The wind that blew up that afternoon was unearthly. It had an evil feel to it – seeming to come from all directions at once.

The sea went from calm to stormy, by-passing the choppy stage altogether. The boat started to be tossed about like a cork. It became impossible to control. The sky swiftly darkened and rain lashed down. Somehow Jesus slept through it. I took charge, as I naturally did in a boat. Some of the landlubbers looked scared - Matthew and one or two of the others didn't like boats at all. But with Andrew, James and John, there were enough of us that knew how to sail a boat through the worst storm. But I hadn't reckoned on a storm like this. I didn't know what to do – a new experience for me on a boat - for I couldn't tell the wind direction. How could we know which way to steer when the wind constantly shifted and sometimes seemed to come from above us, shrieking like a demonic taunt as it did so? A wave towered to our side and broke over our heads. We started to bail and I began to feel a deep, clawing feeling, stronger than the worry that had been creeping up on me. I – who was never afraid in a boat – started to feel fear. I glanced around and saw the same feeling nakedly displayed on the faces of my friends. They were shouting to each other now.

"We should wake him!"
"We'll sink if this carries on!"
"Someone should do it!"

Gradually they all looked to me. I could not believe that Jesus could sleep like a baby through such weather. The boat pitched and twisted and rolled, rising and then plunging into the depths of another wave, all the time taking on more water. They were right. Jesus should be made aware of it.

Holding tightly to a rope, I stepped over to where he lay, reached down and shook his shoulder.
"Master – wake up!!!" The others joined in, shouting their desperate cries over the fury of the storm. "Save us, Lord!" Their fear was palpable. And out of their fear sprang accusations, "Don't you care if we drown?" What an accusation to hurl at Love Personified!

But he woke. He looked around. He remained calm, but his eyes narrowed as he heard the shriek of his enemy in the screaming wind. Sensing the evil intent in the turmoil of the dark, heaving waves, his voice rang out. "Peace. Be still."

He spoke not only to the weather, but to the one who would slay him whilst he slept.

Calm fell. Instantly. Such a thing did not happen. I shuddered. This had been no earthly storm.

His God-given authority stopped the enemy's attack in its tracks. We were astounded, and he turned to us... our accusations still fresh in his mind. All he said, with almost a tinge of sadness, was: "Do you still not trust me?"

We were safe now.

■■■

Meditation

How fickle is our trust, yet he still responds to our cries of help.

The same authority that was his, he has shared with us.

What are the waves that threaten to sink your boat? Is it a freak storm, or could it be an enemy attack, stirred up against you while you were sleeping?

Either way, the solution is as it always was.
He does care if you drown.
He no longer sleeps, but he still awaits your cry for help.

When he hears, "Lord save me!" he will stand. He will utter the words, "Peace. Be still."

Allow the power of those words to sink into your being.
Allow them to still your heart.
Allow trust to rise up.

It will become calm.
Peace. Be still

Poem - Water at the Well

He came to me – the Living Water himself came and asked

"Will you give me a drink of water?"

Me - a woman.

Worse – a Samaritan woman.

Even worse than that - a Samaritan woman living in disgrace and sin.

I tried to argue - "Why me?"

I tried to turn it into a theological debate.

Still he spoke of sources of endless supplies of living water. He revealed himself.

Finally, he looked into my heart and spoke of my sin. No condemnation in his voice. Just the offer of fresh, living water, to wash away my sin and give me the life I was looking for.

He didn't need water.

He wanted me. To deposit his very Spirit into my being.

"Will you give me a drink of water?"

That was his question then.

Now he asks it differently.

"Will you come?"

From Despair to Deliverance

The enemy was spitting mad - Jesus just withstood everything that could be thrown at him. The encounter in the desert, the violent storm – his plots were foiled. And now his latest ploy of tossing criticism at Jesus using, not just the Pharisees, but even the friends of the Baptist, had fallen flat.

It was time for more action beyond words. The enemy knew that stories about Jesus' healing power were spreading far and wide. He sneered. "So he likes to heal... well, let's inundate him then. See how he copes with pressure." And he reached out to steal the life of a little girl. His demonic companions – the black raiders - delighted in his viciousness.

But they didn't count on the girl's father. A man used to power, he recognised a leader when he saw one. A synagogue ruler, one of the religious ones. But not too proud to ask Jesus for help. He got to his knees. "Come," he begged. Jesus rose. Compassion in his eyes. A steadying hand on Jairus' bowed shoulder. They walked together to the house where the girl lay dying.

How easy it would have been, how great the glory, to simply save his power for this glorious miracle. The child of one of the synagogue rulers healed! Surely that would be the only news worth hearing that day. What else mattered? But each and every one mattered.

Even the woman no one wanted to know.
She was alone most of the time.

She thought about God sometimes. Thinking of Him was all she could do - she was not allowed in His house. For twelve long years she had been forbidden entry to the synagogue. She was unclean. The bleeding she suffered from was not severe enough to kill her, but it was constant. Some days she wondered if she would be better off if she did bleed to death.

At first she knew it was not her fault, but gradually, as the bleeding persisted - hidden but known - a sense of shame grew inside her as, one by one, family and friends deserted her. She didn't blame them. If they sat on a chair she had sat on, they became unclean too. It was the same if they touched her 'unclean' bed and, likewise, if they touched her. For them, were they to do any of these things, they would then have to wash all their clothes and bathe, and not until evening would they become clean again. If she forgot to rinse her hands before touching a clay pot, it had to be destroyed. Anything or anyone she touched had to be washed. But no amount of washing could clean her.

By now, the whole town knew her guilty secret. They had seen the healers come and go. All the money she had spent on promised 'miracle cures' had been in vain. She remained afflicted, and had no money now either.

It was shameful. She must have done something wrong... otherwise, why would God not heal her?

When she had to venture out, people steered clear lest she brush up against them. The traders hated to serve her... even touching her coins would make them unclean. So she went out as little as possible. But today, the rumours had reached even her, for Jesus' fame was widespread.

What if he really could heal? Oh, she dreamt about the possibility of that! She was desperate enough to try anything. She could no longer go to the synagogue to approach God – she was too unclean - but she could approach this man.

So she ventured out. It was crowded. People were pushing and shoving to get close to him. She dared not walk up to his face, but she did dare to approach him from behind. She gathered he was on his way to heal a child. A twinge of hope stirred. If he is a healer, maybe I just need to touch the hem of his garment….perhaps, if this man were a miracle worker, his clothes would contain the healing power too. It was logical. Of course she knew that he would become unclean if she touched his garment - but without eyes in the back of his head, he would never see her – he would never know.

She started to press into the crowd. She was unaware of the raider by her side. When she saw the masses pushing and shoving, he whispered, 'you'll never get through'. He nudged her in the place he knew caused her pain and urged her to 'give up now.' All she knew was pain and a weariness, a hopelessness as she saw the crush around Jesus.

But she did not see the angel. The angels liked to hang out around Jesus. It was never boring, watching him. Diligence moved in to lend a wing. She eased it between people, commanding: "Make a way! One coming through!" Risk lifted a wing behind the woman and urged her closer to the one in the centre of the crush. The raider shrunk back in fear and the woman found herself at the front of the crowd. Jesus had his back to her, but he was just a hand stretch away.

Someone recognised her, even as she approached – and word spread that she was there. People drew back. No one wanted to accidentally brush into her. As people drew away she edged nearer, bit by bit, until Jesus was within reach.

She had come too far to change her mind now. He would never know. And she stretched out a hand and touched the hem of his garment. And she was healed. Instantly.

The entourage en route to Jairus' house almost fell into a heap as the momentum was broken by Jesus stopping still. "Who touched me?"

People slipped into instant denial. "Not me, not me".

She hid, trembling. Surely they wouldn't think it was her – there were so many people around, pressing in. The same thought occurred to his friend.

"Master, everyone is touching you!"

What was the problem? Everybody waited for Jesus to move on – had he forgotten a child was dying?

But Jesus remained still and his insistent question cut across their words. "Who touched me?"

His eyes scanned the crowds, searching her out. Still she dared not look at him. He would not move on. "Who touched me?"

The shame and blame of so many years refused to die down. It rose up in her heart. The guilt became unbearable.
She threw herself on the floor at his feet. "It was me..."

Hesitantly at first, she confessed that she had dared to steal his power and yet, it had worked. She could feel the bleeding had stopped. But she was a thief now as well as an outcast. And she had made him unclean. She was healed, but she was still ashamed. She was scared of his anger. She was almost cringing, waiting for his rebuke.

"Daughter, your faith has healed you. Go in peace."

Daughter?? Daughter?? He was not cross! His voice was soft and warm. The words were spoken with real affection – she could hear it in his voice. He was not ashamed to be touched by her, she realised. He had called her 'daughter' as if she were adopted. The thief persona, the outcast, was banished. As Jesus spoke the words of the Father, the sense of being wanted, of being adopted, fell over her like a warm blanket. And he said she had faith!? She who had not been near a synagogue for twelve years!? Her heart overflowed and peace flooded her being. She dared to look up and his warm smile, the look in his eyes, was something she would always remember and treasure. His look of love, acceptance, approval, was aimed directly at her.

And she realised that her fears were unfounded – nothing could make him unclean, nothing could pollute him. Instead of her making him unclean, his purity and righteousness had cleansed her from the bleeding, cleansed her from the deep shame. She was washed. She was new.

The raiders were snarling now. They had hoped he would ignore her, or scold her, but no. Another of their victims who they had taunted for twelve years was snatched from their grasp. They just hoped she had drained him of power. And then they heard the wails. The encounter had at least stolen precious time. Time enough for the true thief to steal the child's life. They sniggered, hugging themselves as they knew Jesus was out of time. He had failed.

But Jesus continued to Jairus' house, unfazed by the news of the child's death. "Don't be afraid," still his hand was warm on Jairus' shoulder.

The enemy frowned as Jesus proclaimed the words that the child still only slept. He, Satan, owned the realms of the dead, didn't he? What was Jesus up to? He couldn't be planning on trying to heal the girl, could he? He only let his closest friends and the child's parents remain. If he was planning something big, surely he would want the masses to see, wouldn't he? He wouldn't shun fame?

Yet Jesus followed the ways that only those with compassion and love can hope to understand.

There were just six people in the room, plus the lifeless girl. Oh, but there was a crush of angels. Young Pip in the midst quite forgot he had wings, and jumped up and down. "Let me see! Let me see!" Glory smiled indulgently and dryly muttered "wings" to him. Pip sheepishly remembered, beat them, and rose up to hover in the suddenly still air. His eyes were fixed on Jesus. His heart hammered.

Jesus spoke to the girl. She stirred. She stared in wonder at him and was caught up in the embrace of her parents. The weeping was silenced and joy swept through the house. A cheer rose up and angel song filled the room. Pip was turning somersaults in mid air and the room throbbed with glory. The child was raised from the dead. Raised to life! Alive!

The enemy was shaken. The raiders couldn't understand. The girl had died, hadn't she? How was she alive again? They looked to their master for answers. He had none. Furiously he schemed. This man foiled every scheme of his.

And the King of Love refused the crown of fame, and continued to hang out with people, showing them the heart of God wherever he went.

••

Meditation

Think about the different characters in the story. Which one do you identify with?

The woman... imagine you like her - daring to approach the miracle man. Dare to reach out and touch the hem of his robe... dare to admit your need of him. Allow him to cleanse you, heal you... allow his acceptance to wash away the shame.

The crowd. Frightened of someone so desperate and unclean, shocked and dismayed with the woman's boldness, yet perhaps envious, too, for she was the one who received the blessing. Does his mercy extend to you too? Why not reach out and touch him, confess the hardness of your heart which threatens to deaden the hidden desire to know him more closely.

Or Peter? Peter was eager to get the work of God done, but did not quite see what the work of God, at that instant, was. Do you sometimes brush over the little things or the little people in your desire to see the big things of God? Jesus loves the desire, Peter was one of his closest friends. Tell Jesus about your impatience, your burning desires.

Jairus. Overcome with desperation and grief. Unable to talk.

His daughter. Dead to the world.

Listen to the words of Jesus. I believe they apply to each of these characters. Know that his words are for you, too, as you come to him, "Daughter [or read 'son'], your faith has healed you. Go in peace".
Allow his words to go deep. Believe that the love in his eyes is for you.

Poem – Jesus came

The Bible leapt to life.
Prophecies that were words of hope
now fulfilled.

Emmanuel – truly, God was now with us.

He chose
not only to come, but to be with us
in all our states.

From toilet training through childhood
He was with us. He was our friend.
Never failing to pour himself out in love.
He showed us that God does more than speak –
His very presence with us
Interested in everything from
carpentry to discipleship,
fishing to preaching,
and weeping with his love for the world.
He came and showed us
that even death is not final.
That there can be joy midst deepest sorrow.
That everything is possible.

That there is always hope.

Lydia's Story: Encounters with Jesus Part 1

They sat side by side on a grassy bank that overlooked the vast crystal sea.

I cannot say exactly what they looked like. They resembled the way they had looked on earth, yet they were different. All lines of worry, stress, fear and pain had been smoothed away from their faces and now those faces seemed to shine as if from a light within.

I cannot say how long they sat there gazing, for time in heaven is not linear as it is on earth, and measurement is meaningless.

On earth they would have made strange and unlikely companions. But here they sat, side by side, in complete unity, although they did not know one another. A shared love united them. A shared Spirit.

Eventually the man spoke to the beautiful young woman. "So, where did you meet him?"

She smiled, remembering, and told her story.
"In a field, on a hill. I was just a child. My father was a rich cloth merchant. He was curious about Jesus and went to see him. There were crowds there, of course, and many other children, but most of them were poor. The sort of children I wouldn't normally be allowed to mix with. I had to play with children of my own status. I didn't know what that meant except that it was a sort of play that was very correct and formal, and was no fun at all. We weren't supposed to run, or get dirty or rip our clothes. Far from looking down on these poorer children, I envied them. My father only took me because my mother was feeling unwell that morning and begged him to take me. No one else was around to watch me, so he reluctantly took me with him. He told me to sit on a tree

trunk whilst he pushed through the crowd to get a clearer view of Jesus.

So, obediently at first, I sat. I sat and watched the poorer children playing. They had small sticks, and were using them to hit large nuts to one another. They ran and fell and squealed but, above all, they laughed. They were having the sort of fun I could only dream of. They bored of the game quickly and then started to play a game involving tagging one another. Those who hadn't yet been tagged ran from those tagging, hiding behind trees or trying to lose themselves in the people milling around. Then a small, scruffy girl ran in my direction. Her face was red with excitement and she was looking for somewhere to hide. When she saw me she stopped abruptly. Despite her young age, she knew the social boundaries.

But I smiled at her and said, 'Quick! Hide behind me! They won't look here!'

She hesitated, looked behind her and then swiftly moved behind me to crouch down behind my back.
"What's your name?" I hissed.

"Ana," she replied softly. "What's yours?"

"Lydia. Sssssh, they're coming."
The other children drew closer, but hesitated when they saw me there. I was dressed in very fine clothes, for my family always had the pick of father's finest material. It was a way of showing off his wares as well as his status. But the poor children were wary of wealth, and turned away. They knew I was not one of them.

"They're going away," I hissed to Ana. I knew my father would not even approve of me talking to her, but he wasn't here right now, and I was bored as well as envious of the fun these children were having. Ana and I started to whisper together. She kept giggling at

29

the wonderful secret of her excellent hiding place. She had the happiest giggle I had ever heard.

Eventually the other children returned. There were more of them now. The taggers had found and tagged everyone except Ana. A tall boy was looking in all directions and he called out, as loud as he dared, though the adults were paying him no attention anyway. "Ana. Come out now. You've won."

"That's my brother, Nathan," she said, rising. "I'm here!"

Her call brought them all over and she laughed in glee at their astonished faces. How they stared!

"Lydia was hiding me!" she declared, holding my hand tightly and pulling me to stand up, defying them to object.

It was Nathan who shrugged. "Ah well," he said grudgingly. "Very clever. What shall we play now?"
Another boy walked up, hearing the question – he was clutching a misshapen ball. It looked like it might have been made of some sort of animal part, but I didn't look too closely. "Kick the ball?" he suggested.

Nathan nodded. He was clearly their leader, and probably the oldest boy there. "Boys against girls," he announced.

They started to move off but I pulled on Ana's hand and asked, "Can I play?"

She looked at me in surprise. "You want to?" I nodded vehemently.

"Come on then," she pulled me along and called out, "Ana's on our side too." A few of the girls stared, but by now the boys were racing off with the ball and no one objected.

30

I was not used to running, but I wasn't going to show it. I raced along with them. My little headscarf flew off very early on, and soon I had hitched up my - by now dusty - skirts which were impeding me.

I got nowhere near the ball until one of the boys accidently kicked it in my direction. I stopped it with my foot, and one of the girls cried out, "Lydia! Here!" Quickly I kicked the ball towards her and as it flew away, one of the boys, a rather fat one, cannoned into me, determined to get the ball. He was too late for that, but still he knocked me clean off my feet, lost his balance and landed on top of me as I skidded along the ground. I banged my head badly on the hard mud and heard someone scream. I lay stunned and winded, realising it was me who had cried out. I was horrified. I expected to see my father storming towards me, but only a few adults nearby glanced around at my scream, and then turned away again. They must have thought it was just one of the poor children.

Ana, my staunch ally, was at my side, pulling me up.

"Lydia, are you alright? You're hurt! Joshua, you oaf!"

Joshua had picked himself up and was dusting down his legs. Had it had been one of the other girls he probably would have shrugged it off. As it was me, however, and my fine blue tunic had a long tear down the side of the arm, and I was covered in mud from the puddle I had skidded through, he looked a bit shame-faced. "Uh, sorry..." he muttered.

Nathan came up. He looked worried and watched me cautiously. I was sitting up now, still catching my breath. I twisted my arm around and saw the long graze beneath the torn sleeve. I winced, but I held the tears back. I might have screamed, but I was not going to cry in front of them. I was desperate to belong. Shakily I stood up, uselessly brushing at the mud down the side of the skirt. I looked around. "Where's the ball?"

But Ana reached for my arm and asked again, "Are you alright? That's a huge graze."
It was stinging, and blood was beading up in the many little cuts. I swallowed the threatening tears, and nodded. "I'm fine," I said. I could hear the tremor in my voice and hoped that no one would notice.

Another girl, whose name was Ruth, came up. She was about my height and looked at me in admiration. "You're everso brave. My big brother would cry the house down with a graze like that." Some of the others nodded.

I smiled weakly. Nathan was still staring at me, and I thought I saw a look of appreciation cross his face. "I've had enough of ball," he said, possibly for my sake. Despite wanting to be brave I was grateful. I was having more fun than I'd ever had with children my own age, but even so, I was tired of running and my arm was hurting.

We sat down in groups on the grass. The number of adults had not diminished. If anything there were more of them than ever.

"How much longer are they going to be?" groaned one of the boys.

"Ages," said Nathan. "They all want to hear him or talk to him, and he'll be here all day at this rate."

"Why is everyone so curious about him?" I asked. My parents had never discussed Jesus in front of me and all I knew was that he was some sort of Rabbi.

"Don't you know?" asked one of them, but I shook my head.

"He does miracles. He makes people better. And he's clever. My father says he's more clever than the Pharisees!" It was Joshua who spoke.

"Have you ever seen him? I mean, up close?" I asked, curious. He shook his head.

"Has anyone?" I asked. There was a mixture of shrugs and shaking heads that answered me. So I said, "Why not? Shall we try?"

It was Nathan that spoke up. "She's got a point. Let's see if we can see him."

One of the girls sneered. "Don't be silly, they won't let us through. We're just children. We'll get into trouble."

"We're small," argued Nathan. "We can slip through the crowd."

He stood up decisively. "Who's coming?"

"I am!" I shot to my feet and winced at the pain in my side, where I had fallen. I would have bruises tomorrow. I was not wary of strangers in a crowd, especially when they were so poor. They wouldn't dare to tell me off. I was more worried about my father who was in there somewhere too, but there were so many people he probably wouldn't see me. Ana stood up by my side, as did another boy and two girls I didn't know. The rest stayed there.

We moved towards the crowd and started to push our way in. It was easy at first, but became harder the nearer we got to the centre.

A woman grasped one of the girls on the shoulder. "Maria! What are you doing here?"

"We just wanted to see Jesus, Mama."

The woman looked down at her daughter, hesitated and then said, more to herself than us, "Why not?" She smiled at us. She looked poor and was very badly dressed, but she had a kind face. "Follow me, then. Stay close." She raised her voice and started grasping people by the shoulder to pull them apart.

"Excuse me, I'm coming through with some children. Let them through, please..." Her voice had a ring of authority and, to our amazement, a path cleared for us. She was joined by a rather severe looking man who I later found out was Nathan and Ana's father. He scooped up Ana, put her on his shoulders, and continued to press forward. Swiftly we moved through the crowd until we could actually see Jesus, sitting on a stone in a small clearing. He was talking to those nearest to him, but looked curiously in our direction as we approached.

At that moment, two huge burly men stood in front of us. One of them said, in a gruff northern accent,
"What are these children doing here? They'll be trampled underfoot! You'd better get them out of the way."

But before he could say another word, and before Maria's mother or Nathan's father could argue, the voice of Jesus rang out.
"Let the children come to me. Don't stop them." He went on to say something about the Kingdom of God belonging to children like us, but I didn't understand. Then we were brought forward to stand in a group before Jesus. I stood near the end of the little line as, one by one, Jesus took us into his arms and blessed us. As I waited for my turn I glanced around. I felt a little awkward. Despite the mud and the torn sleeve, I seemed out of place. My clothes were of good quality – far better than those of the nameless scruffy urchin standing next to me in the line. I looked at the grown ups and then, to my horror, saw a silver silken hat that I knew only too well. It was my father. He had made it to the

front row, and our eyes met. I expected him to be furious – he hadn't wanted to bring me in the first place. But he was smiling. I saw him nudge a man next to him and point to me, as if he were proud that I was his daughter. Before I had time to wonder, it was my turn.

I felt suddenly shy as I stood before Jesus. He looked very grown up and serious. Then he smiled into my eyes and it all changed. I no longer felt out of place. I looked at him and felt that I belonged. I saw he was glad I was there. There was nothing I wanted more than to be held by him right then. My arm suddenly stung as if to remind me that it hurt, and I felt the tears welling up again.

Before they could spill over, Jesus had picked me up, and I sat on his lap feeling suddenly warm and safe.
"Lydia," he said warmly, and I wondered who'd told him my name. He put a hand on my head and prayed quickly and very softly in Aramaic. The odd thing was that, as he prayed, I heard a voice in my head, or maybe in my heart, saying, "You will be a fine woman who knows my heart. My friends will be your friends. You can talk to me at any time, and wherever I am I will hear you. You will always have a place in my heart, for this is where you belong – with me." The voice ceased. I felt so warm inside. Jesus held me tight for a moment, kissed the top of my head, then put his hands around my waist and set me gently back onto the ground.

One of his friends ushered me back to the crowd where my father met me. He took my hand and led me back through the crowd. Twisting round, I exchanged a brief wave to Ana, whose father led her away in a different direction.

As we reached the edge of the crowd I saw something blue hanging from a tree branch. I pointed and cried out, "That's my headscarf! I lost it!" My father paused, reached up, retrieved it and tied it around my hair.

I watched him carefully. Any moment now he would see what a mess I had made of myself. I glanced down and noticed to my surprise that the mud on my dress had been completely brushed off. Apart from a small amount of dust on the hem, it was spotless. I twisted my arm around and gasped. There was no tear in my sleeve. Quickly I pushed it up and found no broken skin. My arm was a little red, but the long graze had completely gone. I looked up at my father with wide eyes. He looked at me. Really looked at me. He was normally a busy man, with little time for children – especially girls - even if I was his daughter. But now he knelt down until he was on my level and said softly, "What is it, Lydia?"

"Jesus!" I exclaimed, my voice shocked. "It's Jesus! He... he... who is he, Papa?" I couldn't explain about my arm. I was too surprised. I felt my side, where I had landed, and the pain there had gone too. I felt warm all over, like I had when I had been with him.

My father did something even more unusual than look at me. He picked me up – something he hadn't done since I was very small. "I don't know, sweetheart..." He had never called me that before!

"He is very special, Papa... I think he is very special."

My father did not answer, but he carried me all the way home. I would like to say that from that day forward he was the warm, loving father I ached for. I would love to report that now I could play with whoever I liked. That my life changed dramatically. But it didn't. My father became absorbed in his work again, and my life was strictly lived in accordance with the social etiquette of the day. Yet something had changed. My father was no longer impatient with me. Sometimes he would look at me warmly, even with curiosity. That moment with Jesus had changed something.

There was an unspoken closeness between us now. My mother had no more children, and when my father died he left me the family business. He had instructed his friends and contacts to trade with me which, with me being a woman, was an unusual gesture to have made. And then I was free. Free to be friends with whoever I chose. But above all, I chose to be friends with Jesus. By now I was convinced that the title they had mocked him with as he died – King of the Jews – was actually who he was.

I continued to talk to him in my heart and I pledged to serve him in his kingdom. I made friends with his friends. To the disgust of my neighbours, I made friends with the poor. I knew from that day when I was a child that Jesus loved the poor. He had time for them, and so would I. I opened my home for any who would come to pray to him. As a gesture I decided to specialise in the colour of the King – I became well known for my trade in fine purple linens. It was the best purple linen to be found in Jerusalem, fit for my friend, the King. This is how I met Jesus."

Meditation

Imagine you can grow down and be a child again. As a child you are taken to meet Jesus. Imagine crawling into his arms to receive a blessing. Do you need healing? Allow his hands to rest on your head as he blesses you.

How were things in your family? Did you ever feel like you didn't fit in? Did you experience rejection? Jesus accepts every child with open arms. He shows people what the Father is like. He removes the sting of every pain. Spend time in his healing presence.

Poem - Peter's song

The tide is turning
Waters churning
How can I leave the boat?
It's safer here
There is no fear
I'm sitting so secure.

A voice in the darkness - "Come"
I know that voice... it's you
It's You - my Friend
The One I follow
My Inspiration
The kindest man
The Wisest
The only real Man I've ever known.

You told me to come once before
and I followed and found life
Real Life.

Moonlight kisses you
and now I see you standing on waves
love in your eyes
power in your being
laughter like foam-capped surf in your eyes.

My legs move, regardless of my reluctant brain
I step out of the boat
suddenly to find
The boundaries that have held me safely
have hemmed me in
Kept me back
Trapped me -

Now I am free to roam the ocean
The mighty sea.

Knowing your grace
Feeling the wind on my face
I look around
hear the sound
of the thundering sea.

The tide is turning
The waters churning
and now I am thinking
"my feet are sinking"
now I am frowning
fear grips - can I be drowning?

Scary sea
Swallowing me
Wind and waves
out of control
Over the roaring noise
Who will hear my cry of help?

Suddenly your strong hand reaches, grasps, holds mine
I can stand again
As I fix my eyes upon Jesus
Your gentle rebuke
"Don't doubt"
warms my heart.

The hand that heals
the hand that fed thousands
The hand that was pierced
The hand that blessed children
and touched lepers - holds me.

Everything is churning
The tide is turning
But hand in Yours, eyes on You
I can walk on water.

Martha Part 1 – Martha

They have gone now. This is a house that has seen much. I sit here and the scenes replay time and again in my mind, as if they happened one after the other in quick succession. The months that separated his visits fade away. Every word he ever spoke seems louder now than it did at the time.

He came with his friends. As he approached that first time it was as if joy were his greatest friend. His smile lit up your heart and his friends hung on his every word. There was so much laughter in the house you could almost taste it. It greatly confused me at first.

His second visit was so different. Instead of joy was a grief so profound that I couldn't understand how the sun could still bear to shine down on him. A time of weeping. A time of shock. A time of awe.

And the third visit. It was a visit of joy and grief mingled. Perhaps overall it was love that stamped itself on our hearts more than ever. I can still smell its sweet scent. The house is full of it. I hope it never fades.

In that hope perhaps now is the time to write. To record those visits that have seared my heart and changed me forever. He has gone now. The house is quiet. Mary went with them. I stay with Lazarus, who is resting in his room. I sit by the window, thinking. I look outside and am transported in my imagination to that first visit...

Part 1

Again I looked out of the window. Where was Mary? We'd both risen early as there was much to do. There were many hours before our visitors were expected, but I wanted everything to be perfect. I needed Mary's help. Really, where was she? Such a dreamer, that girl! How long did it take to collect some herbs? I shook my head and returned to the kitchen. Again I ran through the list in my head of all that needed doing. It was three hours after dawn now, and the sweet, rich smell filling the kitchen suggested that the second batch of bread was nearly ready. The servants had filled the water jugs and prepared some of the food in advance, but I wanted the family to do the bulk of the work. I knew that for the family to serve him gave him more honour than if we left it to the servants. I had come to admire this man from a discreet distance, and I wanted to honour him. I was also curious, of course – I'd never seen him up close, and wanted to be able to be around him and his men. I heard voices and sighed in relief.

"In here", I called.

Anna, Maria and Sara appeared, each carrying baskets. They lived nearby. Anna and Maria were sisters; Sara was their cousin. We were good friends, and would often come to each other's aid when help was needed. Frequently we shared celebrations, but on this occasion they had come to help.

"Was the market busy? Did you get what was needed?" My questions shot out anxiously, before I was struck by my own rudeness. I had failed to give the most basic of greetings. But we had seen each other just late last night as I had laid out my plans and given them lists of things to collect fresh from the market this day. I hoped they knew me well enough to excuse my abruptness.

"Martha," sighed Anna. She was older than me, the oldest of the three of them, and a stickler for the ways of our society. "Are you well this morning? How is your brother, Lazarus? And Mary, is she well?"

"Anna, everyone is just fine. Forgive me, I hope you are all well – indeed I can see you are. I hope your parents are, too. But really, there's so much to do today. We must be ready in time, and my mind is full of arrangements and plans for our honoured visitors. If I'm short on common courtesy, you surely understand why. It in no way reflects disrespect for you." I was desperately trying to curb the impatience that I suspected was in my voice.

Anna made a sort of snorting noise from the back of her throat as she put down her baskets. "Just you mind your manners when these 'honoured visitors' arrive. You cannot greet them so casually if they are to be as honoured as you think."

Sara giggled. She was younger than Mary and apt to be frivolous. "Oh Martha," she said, nervously. "I do hope you're right about them. There are so many rumours about them. Papa was telling us when he returned home last night. He says that some of them are just rough fishermen from Galilee."

Maria nudged her sister. "Hush. You know as well as I do that Rabbis attract all sorts of followers. Why do you always repeat the worst things about people? Papa also said that the Rabbi himself was most unusual."

I was by now checking the produce in the baskets. I passed a basket to Maria. "Perhaps you can start preparing the lamb, Maria. Mary's getting the herbs for it. So, our guest is unusual...?"

I had, of course, heard this before. I'd heard much about him and his words. I'd even heard snippets of his teaching myself. Of course, women were not generally allowed to be taught, but this Rabbi taught in unusual ways. Like the others, he spoke to the men in the synagogue on the Sabbath, but he also taught wherever he happened to be. I'd heard he taught by the Sea of Galilee, on mountainsides, in the markets – anywhere, really. He'd teach as he went around, choosing not to expound the Torah or talk about the finer points of the law but, instead, simply telling stories. Stories that even the children could enjoy and yet, sometimes, even the adults couldn't be sure what he meant by them.

I had heard him talking one day when I was passing near the temple. I'd heard a voice. I'd glanced around and seen a crowd by the temple, but I couldn't see who was speaking. The voice carried, even though its tone was not harsh but soft. And although it was soft, it carried authority.

"The kingdom of heaven is like a treasure that a man discovered hidden in a field. In his excitement, he hid it again and sold everything he owned to get enough money to buy the field."

I paused. Something about that made me think. If I knew of a treasure in a field, would I sell everything to get it? Or would I just pass by, busy as usual, not quite believing my own eyes? How could something like a priceless treasure be buried in a muddy old field? The extraordinary hidden in the mundane? I looked more carefully at the crowd outside the temple. People were standing, listening, but I could also see that those in the front were sitting on the steps. There were a couple of Pharisees on the edge of the crowd, talking quietly to each other. Then I saw him. Right in the

44

centre. Standing on the steps. Was it him? He looked so ordinary. His cloth was simple, he was bearded and had brown hair like many other men. He did not seem especially tall. And then he looked my way. I took a step back. I don't know what struck me, but I had no doubt now that his was the voice I had heard. There seemed to be a challenge in his look. His words lingered in my mind - 'a treasure buried in a field' - would I sell all just to have it? And then he smiled across the square, and his smile seemed to be for me alone. It was too far away to see his eyes, but I somehow knew they were friendly. This was no ordinary man. I remembered that I was on my way to the market, to buy yeast for the bread I needed to make that day. I shook my head and began to move on. But he spoke again, and I could sense he was still watching me.

"The kingdom of heaven is like the yeast a woman used in making bread. Even though she put a little yeast in three measures of flour, it permeated every part of the dough."

I stopped and returned my shocked gaze to him. How did he know what I was doing? Or was the mention of yeast a coincidence? What would a Rabbi know about bread making? Why would he speak of it, if it were not to get my attention at that moment? It was as if he was saying, 'Martha, I'm talking to you. You're going to buy yeast, but I tell you there is treasure even in the ordinary things. Even in me.'

He was still looking at me, and now he threw back his head and let out a laugh of pure joy. I flushed, discomforted. I looked down at my feet and hurried away, my face burning. I allowed myself a quick glance around the square, and to my surprise realised that no one was looking at me or had even noticed me there. Yet for those short moments it seemed as if it had been only him and me in the square. How could anyone not have noticed?

I went to the market, bought my yeast, and made my bread. But his words and his look haunted me all day. I could not put him out of my mind, though I tried. Mary came in later, and she was full of talk of him.

"Oh Martha, he is wonderful! He was teaching in the town today. You should've heard him. He spoke to anybody, not just the Pharisees and Priests. He spoke to the poor people. His closest friends are just ordinary. One of them is even a tax collector. Some are fishermen. But everyone hangs on his words. Everything he says makes so much sense. And he brings so much hope – he says only a little faith is needed. He says not to worry about touching the unclean things, for it's what is in a man's heart that really makes him unclean, not what he touches or eats."

I smiled. "I bet the Pharisees liked that one!" I said, with a cynical laugh. They were so strict about the law. It was especially hard on us women, who were unclean every month for days and had to be so careful at those times about social contact.

Mary laughed in delight. "But he doesn't care about upsetting them. Some of the things he says! Oh, and Martha," her voice grew more intent. "They say he does miracles!"

"Miracles? What miracles?"

"They say he has cured people. People with all sorts of illnesses, even cripples. They say he has cast out demons. They even say he made a blind person see!"

I stared at her. "Who? Who said this?"

"Some of the women who were there had followed him from the North. He comes from the North, I think. One woman I spoke to said she herself had been healed by his words alone."

I thought about that. I remembered his voice. His amazing voice that had reached my ears through the crowd. It had cut through my mind and penetrated my heart.

Could it be possible? I was curious about something else, though. "He lets women follow him?" This was truly unheard of.

Mary nodded. "Oh yes, though I think it is the men that go absolutely everywhere with him. But his followers include women, even married women, and one of them said she used to be, "she lowered her voice, "a harlot!"

"Mary!!" I was shocked and, strangely, a little disappointed. "Didn't he know?"

"Oh yes. She said he told her to stop sinning, so she did."

"What? Just like that?"

"Yes. But all sorts of women were there. Some of them give money to support him. You've heard of King Herod's business manager, Chuza?"

I nodded. Everyone knew of King Herod's men. Chuza was a fairly well known member of the court.

"Well his wife, Joanna, is among his followers. She gives a lot of money."

I shook my head in bewilderment. She was an important lady of influence. What kind of man would attract both celebrities and prostitutes as followers?

Mary let out a sigh. She seemed lost in a reverie. Eventually she glanced up at me and read my thoughts correctly. "Jesus just seems to attract everybody."

Jesus. Yes, I knew that was his name. As Mary spoke it a strange excitement stirred inside, though I didn't know why. Mary hadn't explained how he attracted all kinds of people and yet, after my encounter with him today, I wasn't entirely surprised that he did.

That was how my knowledge of him began. Mary took to quitting the house early to spend the days getting as near to him as possible. I worried about her. She seemed to be increasingly infatuated with him. Yet somehow I couldn't think of him as a bad influence, though I heard rumours that the Pharisees and priests weren't so sure. But Mary repeated his words and deeds to me, and everything he said made so much sense; everything he did seemed so good.

Mary seemed like a girl in love. I was torn. I was the oldest and it was my duty to protect her. Yet I didn't want to stop her going to Jesus daily, for I wanted to know more, and she was my source. I couldn't go following him myself so openly. What would people say, at my age? Jesus didn't discourage her, and as she told me that they spoke together alone sometimes, I began to wonder what his intentions were. More than this though, slowly yet surely, I began to believe in him. I even became convinced he was a prophet from God, and I had only known of him for a few days.

I wanted to see him at closer quarters, but I was far too dignified to follow him through the town. Then I had a brainwave. I decided to invite him and his friends to our house for a feast. By now, our rather studious brother was also quietly becoming convinced that Jesus was someone special. The fact that Lazarus was there made the visit respectable. I asked Lazarus to pass on the invitation, and was both thrilled and daunted when he came home and casually announced that Jesus would come in two days time.

So here we were, with so much to do and no clear idea of just how many were coming. I was terrified we might not have enough of something or that there might not be enough room, though the house was a good size. I had spent the last two days preparing the dried foods and things that would keep, as well as cleaning the house from top to bottom. Oh, and becoming increasingly frustrated with Mary who didn't interrupt her routine of following Jesus just to help me. I supposed I should be grateful that today she had stayed at home. But any such gratitude had long gone by now, for Mary had been gone so long that she was little help. How much time did she need to get a few herbs?

It was nearly mid morning when she re-appeared with two baskets.

"At last!" I scolded. "What on earth have you been doing?"

Maria's eyes were glowing and she took no notice of my disapproval. Her baskets were overflowing with more than just herbs. I also saw bright poppies, roses and other wild flowers in there.

"Here – I have your herbs. And look at the flowers I've gathered, I can make some beautiful decorations with them, for the table and the room."

"Mary – they are men! What will they care for decorations, so long as their stomachs are full? A good meal is all they require, and we're making them the best of meals. I've even bought lamb, though it's not the Sabbath."

"He'll notice. He notices everything."

Sara interrupted, pausing as she chopped vegetables. "Does he really? Do you think he will notice me? I think I'd be scared if he did – they say he can be quite strict with people."

Mary opened her mouth to answer, but I cut in. "No – we shall not pause to discuss Jesus yet again. There's too much to do. I'm sure you need have no fear of him, Sara, and if you do, then stay back in the kitchen. Mary, since you have collected them, you may as well make your decorations. Perhaps you could prepare the eating area while you are about it."

In truth I'd seen the dreamy look on Mary's face as she'd been about to reply. She could talk about Jesus for hours, and I didn't want the others to become distracted. I knew that I wasn't going to get much sensible help out of Mary this day, so I might as well let her prepare the room. It had to be done, after all, and I privately conceded that she did have an artistic flair for such tasks.

So we worked. Much later the aromas in our kitchen were enough in themselves to feast on. I had gone over the recipes many times beforehand. The first platters of bread, goats' cheese and olives were made up beforehand, but the meat and spiced vegetables were best served very fresh. Once again I went through the serving arrangements with the women, though Mary wasn't paying attention. Her eyes were fixed on the open door and the road beyond.

It was mid afternoon, as expected, when they finally arrived. Lazarus was with them and drew them into the house. The scent of the place was amazing. Mary had brought far more herbs than we needed, and had crushed the excess thyme and lemongrass, putting the bruised leaves in little plates concealed around the room where they released their scents. It was a fresh fragrance, but sweetened by little posies of myrtle flowers that she had dotted around. She had hung light woven silks over the windows which cooled the room and kept the dust and pollen out. I briefly welcomed Jesus and then returned, more flustered than ever, to my kitchen. Why did he unsettle me? I had been confident about the food all morning, but now they were here, a thousand anxieties were upon me. Not all his friends were rough fishermen – some were well dressed and looked quite sophisticated. Maria whispered that one of them was a tax collector! Such a man would be very critical of the standards of our hospitality.

The platters were together on the big kitchen table, ready to be taken through. I waited while the men washed the dust from their feet with the scented water provided. Then I started to carry the heavy platters through with Anna and Maria. Sara remained behind to start assembling the many dishes for the main course. Where had Mary got to now?

I was totally unprepared for the shock of seeing her sitting on a low stool near Jesus, looking as if she was settled there for the afternoon. She caught my eye. I'm sure she must have seen the look of urgency in my eyes, the gesture I made with my head as I nodded towards the kitchen. But she ignored it! Instead, she turned towards Jesus, who reclined, chatting with his friends. He glanced up and smiled at me as I laid the bread down. I ducked my head, trying to conceal my anger with my sister. I tried to catch her eye again, but now all her attention was on Jesus. I couldn't linger – there was more to bring through.

Once the breads were served, Anna took me to one side and whispered urgently to me.

"What's Mary doing in there? Surely she's not going to stay with them while they eat? She can't possibly do so!" It hadn't occurred to Anna that Mary might want to actually share the food with them, but such a possibility had occurred to me, though I had pushed the unwelcome thought away. I'd dreaded her doing something like that but dared say nothing to her. Mary had a streak of stubbornness and could not be thwarted if she felt strongly about something. All this work. All this hard work. I had wanted to impress this Rabbi, this prophet, with the excellence of my house, and here we were, flouting one of society's strongest conventions. My reputation would be in tatters. I felt humiliated that my own cousin had to point out to me what I already feared.

"Of course not. She must come here and help us. I'll get her. I don't know what she can be thinking of. Her infatuation for this man has blinded her, I fear."

I lifted a pitcher of wine and took it through to where they sat. As I knelt to place it down, I whispered into Mary's ear. "Mary. You must come and help us. You can't stay while the men dine. What will people think? You can't stay, you know that. We need your help."

Mary looked at me. Such a look of love was on her face. "It'll be alright, Martha." What did that mean? The foolish child! I knew very well that it would not. It would be gossiped about. Even now I was aware of Sara nearby, looking at us. Her curiosity had overcome her fear and she was bringing through jugs of wine and trying to hear what we were saying. Fuming inside but trying to remain calm, I rose and went back for more wine, planning my next words.

After putting the wine down, I whispered into Mary's ear a second time. I placed a hand on her arm, gently trying to pull her away. "Mary, you must come with me. Right now."

She gently lifted off my hand. She spoke again, with no anger or petulance in her voice. Simply and calmly, with a strange maturity that I had not seen in her before, she said in a low voice, "No, Martha. I'm staying."

Inside I was trembling with anger. I wanted to avoid a scene, but now I noticed that Jesus had grown quiet. I glanced up and my heart sunk as I saw his brown eyes regarding us with interest. In his hands he was absentmindedly fondling a sprig of myrtle - one of the many little decorations Mary had made. I suppose I could have walked away and left Mary there to ruin both her, and my, reputations. But, having met the eyes of Jesus, I could not tear mine away. I was vaguely aware that although some of the men still chatted to each other, those nearest to Jesus had grown quiet around us. No, I couldn't walk away. Even if it showed her up, I had to get Mary out of there. People would at least see that I knew how to conduct my household, even if my sister was foolish enough to flout convention. I held the gaze of Jesus, and could have sworn I saw compassion in his face. I was relieved. He understood. He would help me. I appealed to the only person in the room who Mary would listen to. I addressed Jesus. I spoke respectfully to him, hoping that my tone betrayed none of the petulant anger I felt – really, how dare Mary show us up like this? How dare she think she had the right to sit there with Jesus like a man, but worse - with love and devotion in her eyes? I thought quickly, and decided to appeal to his famous sense of justice.

"Lord, doesn't it seem unfair to you that my sister just sits here while I do all the work? Tell her to come and help me."

He replied, and every word was like a hot sword plunged into my stomach.

"My dear Martha," uttered in complete sincerity, with no trace of sarcasm or irony in his voice. Spoken with an affection I didn't understand – I didn't know the man, yet he spoke as one who'd known me and cared for me for a long time. He continued, and the affection of his first words did nothing to remove the sting of what followed. "You are worried and upset over all these details! There is only one thing worth being concerned about. Mary has discovered it, and it will not be taken away from her."

My face flushed and a lump came to my throat. I swallowed hard and rose, deeply embarrassed. He still looked at me as I rose, regarding me with open affection. But how his words stung! I retreated to the kitchen and the murmur of voices rose again as I left. But, strangely, I no longer cared about whether they spoke about me, or even about Mary. What mortified my heart was the rebuke from Jesus. And what warmed my heart were his first three words. "My dear Martha..." Was I? Could I possibly be his dear Martha? Even as he exposed the pride and selfish conceit of my heart? Even then, could I be dear to him? Hot tears rose in my throat, and I breathed deeply, swallowing them back down.

The rest of the meal passed in a confused haze to me. His words rattled around my heart and mind. I longed for peace and quiet to really consider them. Mary sat and ate with the men, and I no longer cared. All I cared about was that I had been so wrong, and that somehow, unbelievably, I was dear to Jesus. Anna questioned me. "Well? Is Mary staying out there with them?" I simply replied, "yes", and something about my tone, or perhaps my dazed confusion, caused her to drop the subject. She glared at Mary with disapproval every time she went in the room, but I just ignored the subject, staying in the kitchen and allowing the others to deliver the sumptuous dishes.

Hours later, it was all over. We were stacking dishes in the kitchen. I noticed they were all empty and I was glad, but had none of the smug, self-satisfied pride about it that I don't doubt I would have felt were it not for the exchange with Jesus. Perhaps my kitchen would be the talk of the town, the accolades of my cooking spoken of far and wide. Or perhaps the conduct of my sister would be the subject tickling ears in the gathering places. I no longer cared about any of these things. All I cared about was that I had earned his rebuke, and that, above all, despite the need for the rebuke, I was dear to him. The water jars were filled, ready for use, and impulsively I plunged my hands into their depths with a prayer. "Wash away my silly pride, Lord God. Cleanse my heart."

There was movement in the main room and Lazarus came into the kitchen.

"Martha, they are taking their leave. They wish to thank you. What are you doing? Come and say farewell to our guests."

I wiped my hands slowly on a cloth. Somehow the gut wrenching pain of his rebuke had faded. All that remained in my heart was the lingering warmth of his words, 'My dear Martha." I was ready to face him again. I squared my shoulders with a deep breath and followed my brother.

"Here she is!" exclaimed one of the men, and I was vaguely aware of voices raised in gratitude and thanks.

I nodded and smiled in acknowledgement, but my eyes flickered over them, looking for that one pair of warm, brown eyes. There they were. Jesus stood in their midst, looking slender and even small next to one of the fishermen. I remembered his words, days ago, by the temple - 'The kingdom of heaven is like treasure in a field.' He was like treasure, concealed not in a field, but hidden in ordinary humanity. Now I understood Mary's love. It was not the love of girlish infatuation for a man. She had seen the treasure. That was why she loved him. She was ready to sell everything to have that treasure – ready to part with her reputation, ready to incur the disapproval of her sister, her family, the whole town if need be. My anger had turned to admiration for her.

As Jesus met my eyes, I felt once again that he knew my every thought. I was no longer ashamed or embarrassed before him. The words that rang in my heart were 'my dear Martha', and suddenly a joy sprung up within and I could not stop the smile from spreading across my face. It was probably the first real smile of the day from me. I felt it warming my eyes.

Quickly he stepped across the room and took my hands in his, squeezing them as a farewell greeting. Another thing that our society would not approve of, but I found I didn't care about that any more. It was like a jolt of hot lightning travelling up my arms and into my heart. There was no doubt now as I looked at him. Love shone out, and he gave a quiet laugh of satisfaction before letting go of my hands, bowing his head slightly, and turning to go. He had not uttered a word, but had communicated more to me in that moment than anyone had ever done in my entire lifetime. From that moment in my life, if I closed my eyes and thought of him, I could still see that loving look, still feel those hands holding mine.

I stood in the doorway, stunned with love, as I watched them go. Mary appeared at my side and took my arm, squeezing it. There was no discomfort in her manner towards me. No sense that we had argued. I understood. In his presence such things did not take root. Such things don't matter when you are overwhelmed in the presence of love.

"Isn't he wonderful?" said Mary happily.

I nodded, shaking off her hand and instead putting my arm around her shoulder and drawing her to me in a hug.

"Yes, dearest, he is."

He was. He was my treasure. And I was his dear Martha.

■■

Meditation

Imagine you were one of those there. Who would you be? A disciple - following Jesus - or one of the women? Where in the house would you be found? Would you be like Martha, busily engrossed in 'doing'? Or, like Mary, soaking up the presence and words of Jesus? Or maybe you would be in another room, out of sight?

Hear him call your name, to come and sit by him with the others? Listen to what he says. Is he teaching, or does he have something he wants to say just to you? Spend time reflecting on this.

Poem - Senses

I have only ever been half a man.
I cannot hear, I cannot speak.
Oh I can see, and touch, and taste.
I can think. I can see so much.
If I go to the synagogue I cannot hear God.
I cannot speak to God, I cannot speak of God - I merely grunt.
I can see people mocking me when I grunt.
I cannot hear them, but I sense their taunts.
They press around me and surround me,
Crowded - I am alone within my walls of silence.

Today there is excitement in the town.
I don't know why - I cannot hear.
But I can see the townspeople
And the out-of-townspeople - crowds of them.
Mouths opening and closing like eyes blinking.
Hands waving and pointing, people milling and waiting.
Are they mouthing the word "Jesus"?
I have not heard of a 'Jesus'. I could not speak to a Jesus.
Dust approaching, more crowds surging.
Trapped I am within their midst.
I can smell their sweat,
Touching them all around, pressing in on me.
A sudden ripple, then stillness holds the crowd.
A hand grasps my upper arm and pulls
I almost fall through the mass as I am tugged.
A sudden stop and again I nearly fall.
Regaining my balance I find I am face to face with a stranger.
The strangest stranger.
A pool of stillness in His eyes. Eyes still watching... me?
I can see the crowd is talking.
I cannot hear them but they point at me.
They plead with this man - perhaps it is Jesus.

they grab his arm, and try to place His hand on me.
He resists and still his look is on me, calling me?
It surely is Jesus.
He leads me now away from the crowd.
We are alone. Just him and me.
My world is always silent
But alone with this man the silence seems to thump in my heart.
I can see Jesus.
The warmth of His look reassures me when - shock -
He puts his fingers in my ears
I can feel Jesus.
His hands are firm yet gentle
The useless ears I have so despised are touched by his warmth,
Held in his hands... of Love.
His touch - reaching into the place where I lack everything.
My senses - such as they are - reel.
Suddenly, strangely, the need to weep wells up.
The man - Jesus - removes his fingers
I see him spit on them.
Now he opens my mouth and touches my tongue with his spit,
And I taste. .. Jesus.
There is no taste of dirt or ear wax
I taste Jesus.
The ugly tongue that strains to speak and only ever grunts, is still
Stroked by the touch of Love.
Now He points upwards - towards heaven, towards God,
And He speaks, his lips move.
He stands close
And I smell His sweet breath.
The sweetest smell I've ever breathed
Fills my nose, my throat, my lungs.
The awareness of all my many needs,
Fades in the fullness of His scent
I breathe deeply of His sweet perfume
And the smallest murmur crawls into my head.
I hear His gentle sigh - "Ephphatha."

The quietest whisper of the faintest breeze
"Ephphatha"... "Be opened", the words now ringing round my
mind.
I can hear Jesus.
He has filled my senses with Himself.
He has walked into my silent world and spoken
I can hear Jesus.
The deaf-mute walls crash down as he leads me by the hand back
to the crowd.
My mouth opens and words - real words - pour out.
Words of His power and Love fall out, yet he smiles and says, 'tell
no one'
And now I see the crowd - they see me, they hear my words
I hear their shocked silence, and then their roar
As they realise I am whole.
I have been alone with Jesus.
I have touched Him, felt Him.
I have tasted Him, smelt Him
I have seen Him, heard Him.
He has filled me.
I have met God.

John's Story: The Lord's Prayer

I am an old man now. Many of my friends – my brothers - are dead. Many have been killed, some in the manner of the one we all love. But I smile as I think of it – they are with him now. Joy everlasting is theirs.

Like them I used to be a disciple. I suppose I still am, but I have had my own disciples now – though of course they too were his. It has shown me how much patience Jesus had with us in those early days. How little we understood! But how thirsty we were to know more! To know him more!

I loved him almost from the first moment. As a brother, as a friend and, as he revealed more and more of the Father to us, as my Messiah.

Many things I will never forget. I have written them down, and they sit with the accounts of Matthew, Mark and Luke. I wrote from the heart, recording the signs he gave us of his divinity and many of his words to us. But the memories make me smile.

I remember how he would often go off on his own to pray. In the early morning, or late at night, or any time really. It became increasingly difficult to escape the crowds, but he would find a way. He would head up a mountain, into the woods, along the lake, or even across the lake on one occasion!

He would leave tired. Initially we would urge him to rest first, but we soon learnt that his time alone with his Father **was** his rest. He would certainly return looking less weary. I remember well the day when he had been away for some hours and then returned at midday. He had been weary that day. But he returned looking radiant, almost as if he were lit up from some inner light. Later, of course, came the day when he took Peter and I up the mountain with him, when he truly did become lit from within. The day we saw Moses and Elijah themselves – ah, but that's another story.

This day he came back shining and full of life. We knew he had been praying, but none of us ever felt or looked like that after prayer!

One of us – I forget who, now - staring at him, let out a cry from the heart,

"Lord, teach us to pray, just as John taught his disciples."

We were sitting – and lying – under the shade of olive trees at the time. The rest of us looked up in interest, nodding our agreement. Jesus looked around at us. He had that look on his face, as if there was some inner joy in him that the request had caused. He paused long enough for me to wonder if he would decline, but then he nodded decisively and sat down on the ground, looking at us. With a huge smile he threw his arms out on either side of him and declared: "This is how you should pray."

And then he spoke that prayer. I shake my head now when I think how little we understood at the time. His life went on to demonstrate every aspect of that prayer. There was much to talk about in those days, but this prayer is something that always came up when we were discussing prayer. We would try and understand what each part of it meant. I'm sure there are many meanings we've not yet fathomed, many ways of praying it yet to be discovered. For it was not words to be learnt by rote and repeated, as some did with the Psalms. It was, we gradually realised, a way of life.

I have never stopped thinking about that prayer.

It began with the word "Father" - "Abba"

That in itself shocked us, for not one of us would address God in such a familiar way. But we had a lot to learn. It was much later when Jesus would tell us that, if we knew him, we knew the Father. Much later before we understood that we had been adopted, and were now sons of God, our Father. I know now that he delights when our hearts are open and trusting, like a child's heart. The 'Abba' speaks of a trust and intimacy that he desires to have between him and us.

"...in heaven..." the words were spoken wistfully. It was his home. He had chosen to be separated from his heavenly home for now, and I think that perhaps he missed being there every day he walked this earth. The same spirit of heaven was in him, of course, but it was not the same. The words were a reminder to have our thoughts, our desires, on the things above, not the things of earth.

"...Holy is your name..." We nodded at that bit – thinking we understood. Hadn't we been worshipping the Holy God in synagogues all our lives? But he wasn't talking about declarations or religious acts. He was talking about something else. Our God was set apart. He didn't demand forms of worship. He desired us to walk in love.

"...Your Kingdom come..." Spoken by a man who daily ushered the kingdom in, into the hearts and lives of all he touched. He was a walking, talking demonstration of the Kingdom on earth. We had not understood that when he said 'the Kingdom of God is at hand', he spoke of himself.

"...Your will be done..." It was a prayer that lined our hearts up with the desires and will of God. God's will being done is sometimes dependent on whether I choose to do it... Jesus was praying for us here, for our hearts to follow his ways.

"...on earth as it is in heaven..." Again our focus was lifted to the home he missed. A place where there was no sin. Oh, that men would turn from the wicked ways of their hearts. Then heaven would come to earth. It can come now, in my heart, if I agree to follow his ways.

"...Give us today our daily bread..." and here my mind flicks between scenes. I remember the stories I learnt as a child - of manna falling from heaven for Israel as the people crossed the desert. I remember the days when he fed 4000, or 5000, with a few loaves of bread. And I remember that last supper as he passed the bread amongst us and said, "This is my body, given for you." Tears slip down my wrinkled cheeks as I remember the sacrifice of love that he made.

"...Forgive us our sins..." This – coming from a man who did not sin yet chose to identify himself with the fallen world that he loved. Of course it was he – Jesus – who made the way for this part of the prayer to be answered. The temple sacrifices are obsolete now, for the one sacrifice for all time has been made.

"...as we forgive those who sin against us..." He told stories about this, of course. It was a favourite theme of his, for he knew the havoc that unforgiveness can cause in a man's heart. But more powerful than the stories was the way he lived it. He forgave Peter's denial. He forgave all of us for deserting him when he needed us the most. Even as he hung there on the cross he prayed, 'Father forgive them, for they do not know what they do.'

"...Lead us not into temptation..." He had told us about the encounter in the desert with the enemy. He had been willing to be led into that place of temptation, but he would not wish it on any of us. He alone knew how hard it was to resist.

"...but deliver us from evil..." The ultimate act of deliverance was his to fulfil, of course. Evil was struck a fatal blow when he destroyed the power of death. He broke out from the tomb having conquered evil, but for now this world is still ruled by the prince of darkness. He continues to prowl, accusing, robbing, destroying. Yes, Lord, deliver us from evil.

When Jesus grew silent, we too sat quietly for a long time, pondering his weighty words. He had a depth of understanding, of wisdom, of intimacy with the Lord God that filled us with both awe and desire.

My cheeks are very wet now, remembering. It's not just his words and his wisdom, you see – I miss **him** so very much. I have had my friends. I have had my disciples. I have this prayer, and other prayers that take me to a place in the Spirit where I meet the Father of Love. But still, I miss the person of Jesus – the brother, the friend that I love.

Here I am, exiled on this little island, with much time to think and pray. I miss him so. It sounds ridiculous but sometimes I wish – almost pray – that he would pay me a visit here. It's a long time now since he set foot on earth, and we are not to expect him before the end of all time now. I know that. I know I will meet him when I die, and such a time can't be too far away now. But I'm lonely here, and how I would love to meet him and be with him here one last time....

(written before John had the Revelation from Jesus)

• •

Meditation

Read the Lord's Prayer (Matthew 6:9-13). Pray through it very slowly. Let the Spirit lead you to pray through every phrase in a way that is relevant to you and your life. No need to do it all in one go. Take your time. Do it often.

Poem – Quiet Time?

Anguished cry shatters morning's dawn
Blood yet to be spilled reflects in crimson sky.
Tears water earth as a man laments, kneeling
Petitions loud echo round mountain rocks.
Shouts not of anger, but burdened heart released here
With passion freely, wildly loosed in lonely space.
Reverent submission in humble heart, yet screaming
Weighed down by love, so painful now to bear.

Who is this?

Can it be a mad man? Yet no, he is quite sane, I see.
Perhaps a raving charismatic - they get everywhere?
No child I see, though racking sobs are wept here.
Loud cries and tears poured forth are held in Father's hands.

Hush now, peace be, and watch - the son is praying
Pure and strong, no yielding to temptation - not he.
Freedom shrieks and shocks the world's dry spirits,
A man as men were truly meant to be

Jesus.

Lydia, the man, and the old woman still sat on the grassy bank. They were silent for a long time after Lydia had told her story. Eventually, the man turned to the older woman and addressed her. "And you, mother, how about you?"

She smiled at him and echoed his word. "Mother," she said softly. "So many years I waited to be called 'mother'." Had she been on earth perhaps she would have sounded sad. But it was impossible to be sad here. Here her words had peace in them.

"I too met him in a field on a hill," she replied. Then she took a deep breath and told her story.

"Many say that, in our time, families were close knit things. As you know, brothers, sisters, children, parents – we all lived together when we could. They say that we knew how to do community. And for many that was true. But my family was small. My parents had just two children. My brother had a family, but he was in the priesthood and lived apart from us.

My husband died before we could have children. Then my mother became sick. It was a sickness that dragged on through the days and weeks and months. She bled often. Never much, but it was always there. It was a curse for her and for all of us, for it made both her and our small household unclean. I would have moved out if I could, but there was nowhere to go. My brother would not have me, there were no children of my own to go to, and no aunts or uncles nearby. Besides, I had to take care of my parents – my father was old and had weak legs. My mother felt the shame of her illness and wouldn't leave the house even if she was strong enough to do so. I was unclean by association. No one would visit such a house, and no one would mix with us. We lived like this for years. I was young when my husband died, but who would marry me when I came with such relatives? I'm sorry to say they felt like millstones around my neck. Any love I once had hardened into bitter resentment after the death of my husband. My childlessness gnawed away at my insides, and I resented having to look after my aged, sick parents. The only person I had who resembled a friend was Tabitha, who lived in the house opposite ours.

I don't know why Tabitha decided to help us, for I was never friendly towards her. Perhaps it was out of loyalty for my mother, for I know my mother had helped her family when she was young. If mother made bread, she would bake more than she needed and give some to Tabitha's mother. She would make clothes for the many children there, and then later for Tabitha's children, when the girl had grown up and married. Since her illness set in, she was unable to do anything like that – she had so little energy or strength, and I certainly wasn't going to waste our precious resources on neighbours. But Tabitha's husband was young, strong and fit and a talented mason who was rarely short of work. They no longer needed our help. In fact, we were the poorer ones now. I was too proud to accept charity but, when Tabitha told me one day that she had too much mending to do on her own, I was glad to help her with it. It meant money. She took in mending and sewing jobs. She was paid for her work and, when I helped her, she passed on the payment. We kept the arrangement quiet between ourselves, for few would have agreed for me to touch their clothing, what with sickness in my house. I would never have found such convenient work on my own. It didn't bring in much money, but enough to keep us in fish, grain and vegetables, and occasionally a little meat. There would never be enough to pay for the medicine my mother needed.

I was grudgingly grateful towards Tabitha, but I would not say we were friends. I sensed that she pitied me, and I did not want her pity. I was jealous of her large, loving family. I shouted at her children if they made too much noise by our door. I knew none of their names except for Philip, and that was only because my father would sometimes sit outside with him. Philip was about 5 or 6 years old, and had a crippled leg. My father said it made them the same, since he was too frail to walk far, and so he would tell Philip stories as they sat outside. Philip was unable to run about with the others but he would sit quietly by my father. I was irritated even by his presence. He had these huge brown eyes that would follow me as I walked. A little fearful they were, and his nervousness around me made me even more cross. He had a curly mop of brown hair – the curls danced whenever he turned his head. For some reason he annoyed me more than all of Tabitha's other children put together, yet he was the least trouble, and even some help for my father. Were it not for their unlikely friendship I would have forbidden him to come near, but it kept my father occupied and I could not afford to alienate Tabitha too much – I depended on her for my work.

Then came that day. In fact it was Tabitha who had persuaded me to go. For some weeks now, every time she brought me clothes to repair, or came to collect those I had done, she would tell me another story about Jesus. I told her I wasn't interested, but in her excitement she wouldn't stop talking about him. I wasn't interested. "Look what religion has done for me!" I would say,

70

waving my arm towards my house. "Look how this God has blessed me," my voice dark with sarcasm.

For a married woman to have failed to bear children was a shameful disgrace. It was the other reason that no man in his right mind would come near me, even were it not for the burden of my parents. In fact I suspected it was the stronger reason of the two. As far as I was aware, I hadn't sinned any more than the next woman, but was being punished all the same. But Tabitha wasn't daunted, even in the face of my anger.

"Even Daniel has decided to take a break before starting his next job. He'll be there too, so there will be no danger. Miriam, you've not been out of this house for months, if not years..."

"Rubbish!" I interrupted rudely." I'm out nearly every morning." I liked to leave early to get food, when there were fewer people around.

She shook her head. "I'm not talking about shopping. I'm talking about a day away from the house. Away from your mother and father. A day for you to rest. To sit in the sun by the lake. When did you last do that?"

"I don't have time for such things. And I couldn't leave them anyway, so don't waste my time even suggesting such a thing."

But she had plotted. "You can leave them. I've spoken to your father. He says your mother is not so bad this week, and that he could manage for a day – even two. My oldest – Sarah – she will stay at home so she can keep an eye out for them too."

"She's just a child!" I exclaimed in horror. "How can you leave her alone here?"

71

"No, Miriam. She's not been a child for a month now. Now she is a woman."

I was momentarily silenced. Was she that old, then? When had she grown up? It seemed like only yesterday when she was rolling around in the sandy road with the rest of them. Time had passed me by whilst I sat in my world of disappointment and bitterness.

Tabitha went on, encouraged by my silence. "She won't be alone, either. My sister is coming to be with her. Sarah will enjoy being treated like an adult for a day or so. She is more than able to do any fetching and carrying. Seeing that she, too, is unclean this week, you won't have to worry about her being unable to cope with any emergencies." I blushed in shame. Even when she was in a good patch, my mother occasionally had a sudden, short haemorrhage. I hadn't realised Tabitha knew.

"It's out of the question," I repeated harshly.

Tabitha stood up abruptly. Perhaps her seemingly endless patience had at last reached the limit. But at that moment my father shuffled out, calling her name as he came. "Tabitha?" He sounded wheezy today. He appeared, and sank gratefully onto one of the small stools we kept by the wall. They caught the evening sun there, but were in the shade during the hottest hours. Tabitha smiled at him.

"Have you told her our plan?" he chuckled.

I cut in sharply. "If you mean the plot to have me idling away by the lake all day worrying about you, then yes. It's ridiculous and pointless. My place is here."

My father looked puzzled. "Where is your gratitude? We thought a day out would be a pleasant surprise. It's all arranged. Young Sarah will help us if we need it. Get some air, spend time by the lake. If I could walk there I would as well. But your mother would be too lonely then."

"Which is one of the reasons I must stay," I said. The odd thing was that when he mentioned the lake, a picture of it crossed my mind. That vast open space. It was not that far away, but it was worlds apart from the cluttered street in Bethsaida where we lived.

He was shaking his head. "She'll be fine with us."

"But Father - there will be people there. I can't go out among people."

It was Tabitha who replied. Perhaps she sensed an unbending in me, but her patience was back now and she bent her full powers of persuasion towards me. "Well that's the beauty of it, Miriam. So many strangers are in town, all wanting to see Jesus. Yesterday there were hundreds, maybe a thousand or more down by the sea. You'll go unnoticed by any who know you, and everyone else will think you're with us. Which you will be, of course."

"Oh, I hate crowds," I said crossly. For I did. I hated people. People meant happy families. Noisy, smelly, happy families. I wanted to be nowhere near them.

"You don't have to talk to them, or even to us, come to that. We can find you a quiet spot to sit in. It's just one day. We would love you to come."

73

I doubted that, but swallowed the retort. I didn't like people either pleading with me or trying to organise me. My life, such as it was, was bleak and unchanging, but at least it was a life I knew. I wasn't ready to be shaken out of it. I opened my mouth to say as much, but hesitated in the face of my father and Tabitha's pleading eyes. Oh, and even little Philip had appeared now. He too was staring at me with his huge brown eyes, though how could he have heard a word of what had been said?

"Is Aunt Miriam coming too?" he asked in hopeful innocence.

I was shocked to the core. 'Aunt' Miriam? He had never called me that before. He had never called me anything to my face. We barely acknowledged each other, let alone spoke! Now here he was calling me Aunt? He looked at me straight in the eye and asked, "Will you come, Aunt Miriam? Grandpa says you loved the lake when you were a little girl."

What!? Had someone put him up to it? But there was no guile in his expression. And there was hope in his voice. Why on earth would this child want me to come? I would undoubtedly spoil their day. I would get tired and crotchety – I was not used to being around people all day. I would be too hot, there would be flies by the lake, I would be uncomfortable, and I was not one to suffer in silence. I was, of course, used to hearing Philip call my father 'Grandpa' – his own grandparents were dead. But I had no idea my father had been telling him stories about me. I had been silent and open-mouthed long enough. I swallowed and made my reply.

"It seems to be all arranged." I addressed my reply to Philip, for I didn't want my father or Tabitha to think they had won me over. I really can't say why my mind suddenly shifted. It was, after all,

74

just for one day. It was true as well - I had liked being near the lake as a child. It used to feel a little magical. There were smiles exchanged between Tabitha and Papa, and I scowled to see them, feeling somehow tricked.

To pull out now would cause too much fuss, though I considered it more than once over the following days. But two days later I was up at dawn, baking bread to take, bathing my mother and setting out meals for them to eat while I was out. I was genuinely anxious for them. Sarah was too young to be left in charge, although her aunt's presence was reassuring. But they didn't know my parents, didn't know how my mother needed such personal help at times. I knew how to help her move, and how to set her down in the most comfortable way – my father was too frail himself to help much. I felt as if I was leaving them forever, not just having a day out.

"Are you sure all will be well? It isn't too late to say if you want me to stay."

My mother slept on and my father replied,

"We'll be fine. Don't fuss so - always you fuss."

A bitter ball of anger formed in my chest but I didn't reply. So much of myself I gave to them, yet they just accused me of fussing. I kissed them nonetheless, picked up the large basket of bread, and went to the door just as I heard Tabitha approaching.

"Miriam, you're ready?" She sounded a little surprised, as if I might have changed my mind. Just for a second I reconsidered again, but no, I wouldn't stay to be accused of fussing.

"What's in there?" she nodded at the basket.

"Bread," I replied curtly, daring her to object. They might be taking me out for the day, but I was not going to be depending on them for food. "There's enough for all."

But Tabitha didn't object. Her reply surprised me. "Oh, how kind, Miriam. Your bread is always so delicious. We'll pick up some fish from the port to go with it."

Her compliment half-pleased me, but I wasn't entirely sure how sincere she was. Was I being patronised? I half-snorted an acknowledgement as I joined the little band. The children ran ahead, brimming over with excitement. All except for Philip, who couldn't run or even walk very fast or far. He walked for a little while until Daniel reached down and lifted his small son onto his shoulders. He squealed with joy at this, and proceeded to shout out everything he could see.

After half an hour, Philip called out, "I can see it! The sea, I can see it! Papa! Look at the sun sparkling on it! Look at the crowds."

It was true. The lake - or Sea of Galilee - glistened in the morning sunlight. The sun was still rising; the morning was fresh, yet the fisherman would have been back some time by now.

As we approached, we paused by one of the stalls to buy fish, caught and baked that morning. They were stashed away into my basket of bread, which Daniel then carried for me.

It felt strange being with this family. I was so used to being alone. I was quiet for I felt strangely shy, which was ridiculous. Tabitha was occupied in trying to watch the children. The four of them had scampered off in different directions whilst Philip stayed by my side, since his father had placed him down and gone in search of news of this Jesus. Daniel eventually returned looking a little perturbed.

He spoke to Tabitha and I. "They say he was here, but he's gone now."

"Gone? Gone where?" asked Tabitha, her voice full of disappointment.

"Onto the lake. His friends are fisherman – he went off not long ago, in one of their boats. Someone said a messenger had come from Jerusalem with news – I don't know what news, but Jesus left soon after."

I sighed. This was all for nothing, then. Another disappointment. I realised as I recognised that feeling that I had actually been interested in seeing this Jesus. I'd heard much about him, I supposed, both from Tabitha and from odd scraps I'd picked up when I was out shopping. It was rare that anything of excitement happened in our town, and Jesus had certainly caused a stir. I was about to suggest that we head home, but Daniel hadn't finished.

"Although he's left, people seem to think they know where he was headed." He mentioned a place I had never heard of.

"Where's that? I know of no village of that name?"

"There's no village there. It's a barren area of wilderness. But they say Jesus sometimes goes there for solitude. It's by the hills. The thing is, it's not many miles away. We could be there by midday if we set off now."

Tabitha considered it. "The children could walk it, but what about Miriam? She could not go so far."

77

"I'm no invalid. Nor so old that I cannot walk," I retorted. "Of course I can walk it."

A small smile played around Miriam's mouth, and I frowned. Had she goaded me into agreeing again?

"Well, I can give Philip a ride, so let's go, shall we?" asked Daniel, with a smile. Tabitha nodded and started to collect up her children.

We reached the wilderness in the three hours or so that Daniel had predicted. But by the time we got there we were hot and tired, for the sun was up. There were many people on the same road, and when we finally arrived at a grassy plain which was on a slight slope beneath the hills, we realised that many more had come earlier, and from many directions. There were more than a few hundred, I realised in astonishment. Perhaps a few thousand! We sat down on our arrival and shared the food out, for the children were complaining about their hunger. They gobbled up the fish and bread. Except for Philip. He left his share in a little package in the basket.

"Aren't you hungry?" asked his mother.

He shook his head, his eyes shining with excitement. "No. I want to see Jesus first."

I was puzzled. I too was curious about Jesus, but for such a child to be so eager? I didn't understand.

"So why is Philip so keen on finding Jesus?" I asked as he limped away, holding the hand of his oldest brother.

"His leg, Miriam," said Tabitha gently. "Remember, Jesus is a healer. It's one of the reasons we're here."

"What!" I was shocked. "You never mentioned this! How ridiculous! The poor child! Dragged out here for some false hope. How could you think of such a thing?"

"Miriam!" Daniel raised his voice at me and, surprised, I was silenced. The remaining children stared at us. He continued more quietly, but there was still a trace of anger in his voice,

"I will ask you to keep your opinions to yourself. Your bitterness is truly poisonous at times, and I will not have it affecting my children. They have a right to hope that God is good, even if you have your doubts."

I was seething now. Bitter? I supposed I was bitter. Anyone with my lot in life would be bitter. When had God been good to me? I wanted to say as much, but I was aware of Tabitha pleading at me silently with her eyes to not speak. I was angry, though, and realised in surprise that a lump had come to my throat. I swallowed several times. I was simply not used to being spoken to like this. I wasn't used to people. I barely knew Daniel, and here he was rebuking me in front of his family.

I could not stay silent for long. I let out a tirade of complaints.

"Well. If that's how you speak to an invited guest! An older woman! In my day I was taught to respect my elders. But no. I'm told to expect a nice day sitting by the lake, and instead I'm dragged across the barren countryside to the middle of nowhere, where we are pressed in on all sides by hordes of people. All for a false hope that I was not told about...." I muttered on for a while before lapsing into silence.

Daniel had opened his mouth to respond, but Tabitha put a hand onto his arm and he closed it again. He hung his head, listening to me rattle on. I could sense a cloud of unhappiness descending upon us, and suspected that I was the source of it. I no longer cared, however. I was miserable, and if that made everyone else miserable, so be it.

The children wandered off, and time passed. Perhaps I dozed a little, for it was hot, even though we had a little shade from the tree I was leaning against. I woke suddenly though, momentarily confused, as a buzz of anticipation rippled through the crowd like a wind passing over a cornfield.

Daniel stood up and called out, "Philip!" Hopeless. Who could see a small child in the midst of all these people?

"What is it?" I asked.

"Jesus," replied Tabitha. "They say he's arrived. Come on, let's go down to the lake."

I stood up a little stiffly and looked in that direction. The crowds were thicker there. "I think I'll wait here." I said. "I'm tired, and it's too hot to find a way through the people."

Tabitha and Daniel exchanged a frustrated glance. I bet they wish they'd never asked me along now, I thought, somewhat smugly.

"I'll wait here with her. You find Philip, and the others," said Tabitha. Daniel nodded, looking annoyed and worried, but I didn't care. I no longer liked the man.

Daniel returned some time later with three of the children, but not with Philip or his older brother. "I can't find them." He reported. "Perhaps you were right to wait here. He knows we're here."

But it was not long before Philip and his brother found us. We heard shrieks of "Mama!! Papa!!" before Philip and his brother both came tearing towards us in a breathless sprint. Philip was running! His father stood up and stared at the sight of the two approaching tornados, and Philip took a giant leap and threw himself around his Father's neck. Tabitha's hands flew to cover her mouth and her eyes were wide in shock. I simply stared in disbelief.

Philip was shouting out, though, "Did you see? Did you see? I can run now! Jesus came off the boat and just went through the crowd, healing everyone he touched! They'd brought loads of sick people to the lakeside and he healed every one of them!"

"What did he say?" asked Daniel, gruffly. His voice was thick with emotion as he set his son down.

"Nothing. He just touched my head, smiled down at me, and moved on. I felt a twinge in my leg, and when I looked down, it was straight." He stuck out his bad leg, and it was true. It was bad no longer. The foot no longer turned inwards, as it used to. It looked just like the other one. "Look, Mama! Do you see?"

Tabitha had tears running down her cheeks as she knelt and gently ran her hands down his leg. She beamed up at Daniel through her tears. "Dear God," she whispered. "It's true!" Daniel knelt by her and put an arm around her, murmuring into her ear as he held her tight.

81

I was utterly shocked to the core, but no one was asking my opinion. I simply sat and stared.

Soon there was movement in the crowd. Jesus was moving. He passed not far from us, and continued up the hill. How could he have done such a thing? He looked so ordinary. He was making no fuss about having wielded such power. He simply carried on. At some point he stopped, sat on a rock, and started talking to the crowds. He was teaching. Some teach in the synagogues – those temples of purity into which I was too unclean to venture into. I believe Jesus taught there sometimes, too. But he also taught like this, out in the open, to any who would come.

So we listened. He talked a lot about his Father, which puzzled me as I had heard that his Father was just a carpenter. But he spoke about love, and true goodness. He talked about what mattered most to God – not the keeping of all the many laws, but justice and compassion. He talked about forgiveness. About living in peace. Peace. I had forgotten there was such a thing. I barely believed in it anymore. My heart and mind were always in a turmoil of questions and doubts, anger and bitterness. There was no peace for someone like me. No hope. My life went nowhere. And yet, I had thought there was no hope for Philip, but here he was, jumping up and down like a spring before me.

Jesus taught on, for many hours which seemed to pass like minutes. Sometimes he would stop and talk to the big fishermen who were his friends, or else with people whom he had healed.

I was shocked when I saw that the evening sun was sinking. The crowds had not thinned. The children had slept in the afternoon, but now they were waking and complaining about hunger. Philip was sitting at my feet and suddenly stood up, pointing.

"That's one of his friends."

I looked and saw the wiry, curly haired fisherman standing nearby talking to someone. Boldly, Philip who – even this morning - had once been shy, approached the man and tugged at his sleeve.

The man looked around, and down at Philip. "What's your name?" asked Philip.

"Andrew. I'm Andrew, little man. And you?"

"I'm Philip. Jesus made my leg better today. I can run and jump now. Look!" He jumped up and down on the spot. "What's Jesus doing now?" he asked, for the teaching had stopped, and Jesus was simply sitting, watching his friends. Some were standing in a group, but others, like Andrew, had moved amongst the crowd.

"Well," said Andrew slowly, "it's really time for people to go home now, but Jesus wants everyone to have food first."

"What food?" asked Philip.

Andrew paused. "I'm not sure yet," he said. "We haven't actually got any."

Philip stared. "Wait there," he said and quickly turned ran to the basket we had carried from home. He dived in and pulled out his packet of uneaten fish from the bottom of the basket along with the remaining rolls I had made. He rushed back to Andrew.

"You can have these," he said, and then corrected himself. "Jesus can have these. We bought the fish fresh from the lake today, and the bread's fresh, too." Andrew let out a laugh, but he knelt down to Philip's level and said, "Thank you. I'll see he gets them." He moved away, taking the food, those few loaves and wrapped fish with him.

I shook my head as Philip returned. "It's a long walk back home, young man, on an empty stomach."

Philip just smiled at me and replied, "Aunt Miriam, I could run all the way!" There was really no arguing with him, not as he stood there delighted with his new straight leg. Daniel started talking about the journey home and wondering if we could pay one of the fishermen to take us in his boat, but before we could move, a noise grew. We noticed that those who had been near to Jesus were moving amongst the crowds. A woman passed by with a big basket.

"There's food here," she called, happily. "Take some."

When she came to our group I could see the basket was overflowing with bread and fish. There were others going around with more, too. We took enough for ourselves, and there seemed to be no less.

"Where did all this come from?" I asked her.

She just smiled and said simply, "Jesus."

Yet we had heard and seen that Jesus had been empty handed. I started to feel strange. This Jesus, who straightened out bent limbs, also took a child's lunch and seemingly multiplied it. And everyone was invited to listen to his teaching; anyone could share his bread. I had been shut out from many circles of society, yet here I was not only tolerated, but invited to share food. It didn't seem to matter whether I was clean or unclean. Even if I was bitter and ungrateful, I was as welcome as anyone else. My hands shook as I held the bread. I knew little about twisted legs, but I knew about bread. Bread didn't just happen or appear out of nowhere. And yet it had. I took a bite and swallowed. And I was undone. The shock as I recognised the flavour of the bread made me gasp. I tried to hold back the sensation in my chest, but it refused to be suppressed. A huge choking sob burst out. Then another. Then the tears started to flow. Huge choking sobs with many, many tears. Suddenly I was crying out all the years of bitterness and loneliness and pain.

They all stared as I rocked back and forth, weeping with abandon.

Finally Philip himself crawled into my arms – something no one had ever done. It made me cry all the more, and I held him tight.

"What is it, Aunt Miriam?" he asked. Between the sobs, which strangely were turning into sobs of laughter now, I declared, "It's my bread! Jesus has used my bread!"

I shook my head helplessly, unable to say more. Who was this Jesus? I knew without doubt that he had seen me, just as he had seen Philip. Just as he had straightened out Philip's leg with the simplest of touches, somehow just one bite of his bread has straightened out my twisted heart. He had used my bread – somehow that gave me worth. Somehow it made me feel wonderfully loved and accepted. Quite simply, the thought that all of these people were eating my bread, multiplied by this miracle man, filled me with joy. Laughter bubbled out of me like a spring, complete with tears that continued to roll down my cheeks.

The others caught my mood. Philip cried out in delight, "It was my bread too. It was our bread." He threw back his head, giggling, and sang aloud, "Jesus used our bread! Jesus used our bread!" It was the happiest moment I had known for a very long time.

I felt very strange. The tears subsided now, and I felt cleansed. A warm glow filled me even as I washed the bread and fish down with some wine that Daniel had brought. Somehow I felt part of this little family now. I was as caught up in their emotions as they had been with mine. I saw Daniel watching with a look of wonder as he saw Philip race off with the others, and I smiled affectionately at him. He caught me looking, and smiled back. He walked over and held out an arm to help me up.

"Come on, Aunt Miriam," he said. "Time to go." A warm frisson of delight ran through me as he called me that. Aunt Miriam I was for them all, from that moment. So we made our way back to the lake where Daniel did indeed arrange for one of the fishermen to take us back to Bethsaida by boat.

As we waited for the other people who had done likewise, we heard a shout from behind. "Simeon!"

The man helping people onto the boat looked around and replied. "Andrew! Are you leaving now too? Where are you off to next?" It was the same Andrew that Philip had given his lunch to. He was carrying a basket.

Andrew nodded. "Caperneum. The others are just coming." He saw us standing there and noticed Philip's frantic waving. He came over and ruffled the boy's hair. "Why, it's the little man who Jesus healed. And you gave your food, too. Look. See – there were leftovers. This is just one of twelve baskets left over."

Philip's eyes widened, and my reluctance to engage with strangers had somehow vanished.

"Sir," I asked. It felt foolish addressing a fisherman like that, but after all he was a friend of Jesus, and I had an important question." He looked at me, and I asked,

"How did Jesus do that? With the bread?"

He laughed, and shook his head. "Jesus never fails to surprise us too. Come tomorrow, and see."

I shook my head. "No. My mother's sick. My father needs me. They are in Bethsaida. I need to be there."

He nodded, then reached into his basket and pulled out a loaf and two fish. "Here. Give them these to eat. Jesus himself has blessed these, Mother. He has a strange power - some say it's given by God Himself."

Strange. That same morning I would have laughed in derision at such a statement. I would have told him bitterly that I was no 'mother', but this strange glow I felt inside as I had eaten the bread still lingered in my heart. I simply nodded, took the food he offered with thanks, and put it in my basket which had been empty.

The light was fading fast, and it was dark when we reached the shores of Bethsaida. The children were quiet now, no longer running as they made their way wearily up the hill. All except for Philip, who was still dancing around on his healed leg. We parted at my house. I started to formally thank Tabitha for taking me, but she threw her arms around me and we stayed standing for a long time, it seemed, in a deep embrace. I released her and looked into her eyes, and more tears seeped out of the corners of my eye. "What a friend you've been."

I thought of all the mending she had passed my way, realising that she probably left herself short of work at times in doing so. Thought of the times she had sent Philip around to talk to my father, or Sarah to help me with chores. How I had grumbled at children being underfoot, instead of being grateful for the help they gave me. I suppose I had resented them simply for being the children I could never have. I couldn't understand how I could've changed so much in a day, for now I said. "If ever I can help, you know, even in watching the younger children, send them over."

She beamed. Daniel kissed me on the cheek, and Philip stopped his jigging long enough to come over and give me a hug. I said a little ruefully, "I doubt you'll have time to sit with us now that you can run around with your friends." It was said with a warm smile, but Philip took the remark seriously, and thought, with his head tilted to one side.

"Well, I'd love to play with the others sometimes. But Aunt Miriam, I'll still come and visit you. After all, you make the best bread in town. I think maybe Jesus thinks so too, for he used it! And I want to hear more of Grandpa's stories!" He skipped off with a laugh and I made my way inside to greet my parents.

They were awake, and we had a supper of bread and fish. I ate none of it, but sat with them as they ate, telling them of the great joyous healing that had happened to our neighbour's son. They nodded, and I wasn't sure if they really understood. They would see in the morning, when they saw Philip.

I half hoped they would be overflowing with energy the next day – after all, they ate the bread. But no. My father was still frail and my mother grew tired quickly as usual. They were amazed to see Philip running around, though, with one leg as straight as the other. My mother whispered, "You see, I always said God was good. This man Jesus must be from God!" I could only nod, for I felt strange. Peace, contentment, and even joy had remained with me. It was as if I had eaten them, like the bread, but they stayed with me, in my heart, from that day on. I still had my ups and downs, of course, but the bitterness that had eaten away at me like acid had gone for good.

It was a good few days before I realised that my mother had stopped bleeding. She never bled again, though she remained weak. But this meant I was no longer unclean. I called upon the priest to verify this, and it was so. Now I could go to the synagogue, and be with people. Even so, the people I enjoyed being with above any others were my neighbours.

The following year, my parents both died within weeks of each other after developing an illness that swept through our corner of Bethsaida. Younger people shook it off, but my parents both developed bad coughs until they could breathe no more. But far from being on my own, at their invitation I moved in with Tabitha and her family, becoming their Aunt in all but blood. I loved them all by now, although I have to confess that little Philip was always my favourite.

So you see, in a way I never quite met Jesus. We never exchanged a word. But our paths crossed on that hill, and I was changed forever.

Meditation:

Think about Jesus, the Bread of Life. Is he your source of sustenance and nourishment? Read the following poem slowly. Ask him to feed you. Thank him for your daily bread.

Poem - Bread

Can you smell it.....?
Rich and nourishing
Let it invade your lungs
Breathe deeply...

The Bread of Life has risen
Broken open
for all to take and eat

We no longer rely
on Manna to rain from heaven
No more do we scrabble in the dirt to collect it.

Now the Bread of Heaven has walked among us
Take, eat, it is his body
And the bread of The Presence will be within you

But like Manna, take it afresh, daily
Yesterday's bread just will not do
Let Him fill you anew

Hunger no more
The Living Bread gives life forever
Take, eat His words and know Him

And so we pray, with rumbling hearts
Believing and knowing that you will answer
With all the saints we say

"Give us this day our daily bread"

The Tenth Leper

Disaster entered my life as suddenly as the spot that appeared on my back.

My wife asked, "What is that?" as I undressed one night.

"What is what?" I replied, twisting my neck and looking down in vain, trying to see what she saw.

"There's a blotch, a pink spot, on your back. It's new." Both the tremor in her voice and the fact that she didn't touch it alerted my senses. I felt my face flush in a spasm of fear. I pulled my tunic back on. I turned to Hannah, and saw fear mirrored in her face.

"It may be nothing" she said slowly. "But you must go to the priest. To check."

I shook my head in violent denial, but Hannah persisted.

"Amon," she urged. "Think of the children."

I thought of the children and my heart lurched. I could not put them at risk. Slowly, I nodded. She kissed me. A slow, lingering kiss, and I held her tightly, like a drowning man clutching at a rock. She did not protest but I noticed that her arms did not encircle me, but instead remained pressed against my broad chest.

We climbed into bed. I kept my tunic on. We lay side by side, touching slightly, pretending to sleep. Neither of us had mentioned the word that paralysed our hearts with fear. Leprosy.

I have three children. Two boys and little Tabitha. Daniel and Mark are stocky with thick, straight brown hair, which accentuates their large brown eyes. They will grow to be big and tall, like me. Deborah has the wispy hair and grey eyes of her mother, and will perhaps grow into the same slender frame. Early the next morning Hannah and I had discussed what to say. I was adamant that they were not to know of this.

"Abba go to tip? Big long tip?" Deborah had still not mastered the 'r' .

"Maybe," I replied, kissing her nose while my heart was breaking. I tried to shake off the dread. It might be nothing. "Maybe. I go to see a man who will tell me." Carefully, I picked her up by the waist and swung her high over my head until her serious expression dissolved into a giggle."

"What exactly is the job, Abba?" Daniel asked. "Will it take very long?"

I pretended to consider. "It's a large building job. A job for skilled builders like myself. I won't know for sure if I can do it until I see it. It might lead to more work. But it's far in the north."

Daniel looked worried. My father was at the table, and reassured the boy. "All will be well." His voice was gruff with suppressed emotion. Daniel might not hear it, but I did. "We must take the opportunities God sends."

I looked at him gratefully. I had only told him my news that morning. He had been deeply shocked at the possibility that he might now outlive me.

When I first married, though I loved my parents I was dismayed to live in their house with my brothers. I had wanted to move out and build my own house as soon as I married, but my mother had been dying. She asked me to promise to stay there as long as my father lived. I had reluctantly agreed, instead settling for building an extra wing for my family as it grew. Now I was glad that Hannah and the children would not be alone. But I should be there too - it was my job to provide for them. That was, however, no longer a possibility. A leprous builder would never find work, even if I were by some miracle allowed to remain nearby.

I sighed. I was not normally one for introspection. I would wait and see what the priest said. All might yet be well.

All was not well. The priest tutted and prodded and shook his head.

"Surely we can wait the seven days before you decide?" I pleaded. The Levite shook his head.

"No. I've seen it before, many times. It starts like this. You can return if it clears. But I don't think I'll see you back here again." There was no compassion in his voice as he wrecked my life.

"What will I do? Where will I go?"

He named a village not far away. I knew it, of course. I had never been anywhere near it. It was where all the lepers lived. "Tell your family there are those who will even deliver food there. For a price." He knew we were not the poorest of families.

I felt numb as I walked away. Perhaps one day I would be numb all over – people said that that was a symptom. My wife waited

94

with her sister, and she saw the priest's pronouncement in my face before I reached her. She gave a low moan of grief.

"Hush now," I urged, knowing that I couldn't bear to see her break down here. "He might be wrong. For now, it's best to be cautious. Remember the children." The only thing worse than a leprous adult would be a leprous child. I could not bear to stay and prolong things. When I told her where I would be, the strain on her face intensified.

"We'll send things," she said.

I shook my head. "No!" I replied vehemently. "I can still build. Even if it's for the sick, I will still get paid." I could not bear the thought of her trying to help me. I should be providing for them, like a man. As my role of provider got stripped away, so the sense of shame grew a little bigger.

It grew even more as I walked away. I looked at passing people with a new intensity. These may be the last ordinary people I can walk among, I realised. I was going to be an outcast now. As a Samaritan, the feeling was not entirely new. If ever I did work in Judah, I was made to feel the same. This was different, though. With the former it was bigotry that shunned me. I saw myself as the one who was right, and them as inferior. But now I knew I was the deficient one. In everyone's eyes, whether Jew or Samaritan, I would be an outcast, forever unclean. We Jews and Samaritans were forever arguing about the correct place to worship - but now there would be nowhere for me to worship, amongst either Jews or Samaritans. I was under the judgement of God. He was punishing me, and I had no idea why.

It took me two days to reach the leper village. Once I was off the main highway, the roads became quiet. The other lepers watched as I entered, and I tried not to stare at those I saw. Many were obviously disfigured, and once the horror faded I grew used to some of the sights I saw. I learnt to look away from those with the worse disfigurements. The ones I found myself staring at, however, were those who, like me, had no visible blemish. I found myself wondering where exactly on their bodies the disease was. Wondering if they would die before me, or not.

In truth there was little paid work to be had. The only people I could work for were lepers, and few of those had money. But I found work to do all the same. It was more usual to be paid in food and friendship, and I found that life in the village was not the nightmare I had imagined. I started to learn about this illness. There seemed to be many varieties of it. Some people noticed a skin lesion and found that it spread rapidly. Some were dead within a year or two. Others lingered on, becoming progressively worse, plagued with infections, numbness and disfigurements. Some seemed to find their disease halted for months, and then grew worse before halting again. Others again found that it never grew worse, but that they were stuck here, for their original lesion remained and no priest would declare them clean again. What would be worse, I wondered? A swift death, or a lingering one, where one grew uglier by the month, outliving those you knew, watching them die helpless and blind, and knowing that the same fate awaited you? Such thoughts were unbearable, yet they stalked me, especially through the watches of the night.

There was a kind of sick house for those near the end - for those who had no living relatives to nurse them in that God-forsaken place. I agreed to work on the roof, which was in need of repairs.

96

There was little enough anyone could do for those who suffered there, and helping to keep the rain out was something I could do. Perhaps in the back of my mind was the thought that, should I die there, someone might likewise care for me near the end. This was how I met Simeon. I looked at his disfigured face with repulsion and morbid fascination. His sight was gone, so I could study him without him knowing. Or so I thought. But I underestimated his other senses.

"You again." His voice was husky. He had lesions in his throat.

"Again?"

"Ah, you may be sick, but you still have strength – unlike most who visit this house. I hear you approach. I suppose you come to look. To see how you will end up." I started to protest feebly but he waved a twisted arm at me dismissively. "It matters not. We are all the same. You've not been here long. I've been here a very long time. Tell me about the world you've so recently left."

So, in between working I would sit with Simeon, and my words too frequently and painfully strayed back to my family. Sometimes they would tail off and I would close my eyes, picturing their faces, wondering how they were managing without me. How they would be changing. How I would never see them again. My tears spilled over. Simeon knew.

"It's the hardest thing," he acknowledged, sensing my distress. "I used to think that when I was this ill, the pain would be the hardest thing to bear. Or the hunger. Or the helplessness. But it's loss of those I love that cuts the deepest. Knowing I have a wife in this world who walks alone. Or worse, that she doesn't. Or that perhaps she lies sick somewhere, and I don't even know about it."

97

I stared at him, horrified. I hadn't even considered such possibilities. But Simeon had had plenty of time to imagine such scenarios. And I had learnt that he was not so fortunate to have a trade or a family large enough to really care for his wife. He had been a farmer. His property was owned by the farm. His wife would have had to leave once he had gone. He did not know her whereabouts. Or even if she still lived. It was a long time since he had received word from her. Years. I reached out a hand and gently encircled his wrist. It was a deliberate action. It was strange, but although we all had the same illness – or variations of it - we lepers did not touch one another. We knew that we were forbidden any contact with the healthy. The stigma of shame in knowing that we were untouchable to most, however, seemed to spread into our souls. We didn't touch one another. Simeon stiffened at my touch and pointed his face in my direction. "Amon, for a Samaritan, you're a good man," he said softly.

I smiled and replied, "Well, for an old Jew, you don't do badly." It was a rare moment of shared kindness.

Months passed as gradually I tried to accept what had happened. I didn't feel ill. I couldn't even see the patch on my back. I felt as if it was a bad dream. Someone would notice the mistake and I would go home. Yet I remained. The shame of my helplessness grew. The best money to be earned came from begging. Begging was a degrading business, yet I was reduced to it on the roads nearby. They led from Galilee to Jerusalem, so were usually busy. I wanted to be able to somehow get some money to send home. I was tormented by thinking of my dearly loved family. Simeon was right – it was the hardest aspect of this place – knowing that they were somewhere else without you. There was nothing I could do to help or protect them. I knew that at some point a careless or cruel word would be spoken and my children would discover what had become of their father. I cringed just thinking about it.

The feeling of well-being gradually faded though. I had been strong, but slowly I was aware of my body becoming weaker. I was shrinking, or so it felt. Next, patches had appeared on my legs. So I did have it, then. I was a leper. No longer a builder, a husband, a father, a Samaritan or even a man. The sickness would spread, and I would die. I was still at a loss to explain how I had offended God and brought this judgement down upon myself. Perhaps my sin had been pride, but there was none left now and still I was leprous.

Then there was the day when a lesion appeared on my face. There was not even the crudest of mirrors in the village, but still I knew. I knew by the look someone gave me as I walked up to the sick house one morning. I saw Anna, who lived in a hut near mine, by the well. She glanced up, nodded a greeting, then glanced back at my face. Her eyes widened and quickly she looked away. She hurried off. I put my hand to my cheek. I could feel nothing. That in itself was a clue. A small patch of numbness.

I went to the one man I could trust.

"Simeon – my face. Is it on my face?" I'd forgotten for a moment that he was blind.

He chuckled softly. "Amon, how would I know?" But he added. "Does it matter? One day it will be there. Does it matter if it is this day?"

But it mattered to me. I could not say why. It being on my face made it so publicly visible. Having seen others in the early stages of the disease, I knew it would just be a discoloured patch at first. But it was a sign of the shame that encompassed us all. I developed the habit of resting my fingers on my cheek to cover it when I spoke, as if I were thinking. I suppose I fooled no one, but it was instinctive. Now I understood the face scarves and hoods that many chose to wear. The shame of it!

I had been there eight long months when the first wildly improbable rumours of hope reached my ears. It appeared that a man - a Northerner in Galilee - had some ability to heal people. It was impossible to believe or even hope, of course. There was no cure for this. Yet such was my desperation that when a small group of men got together to plan a visit to him, I sat with them, listening.

"We cannot leave here, you know that," rasped Eliob, an older man. His breathing was very bad. "We'll be stoned if we try to get near someone holy in a town."

"I'll do anything," said another. "Anything has to be better than this living death. Even stoning."

Several of them nodded. Another spoke. Mattais was a gentle soul, skilled at helping the most sick amongst us. It had been Mattais who had asked me to work on the roof of the sick house. "I can't go. I'm needed here. And my family is here - we couldn't all go." Even more of them nodded at this. The talk went on. Arguments for. Arguments against.

We Israelites can argue for hours, as we proved on that occasion. We would often discuss anything late into the night. To be discussing an action, rather than some obscure religious matter, or the latest development of our sickness, was a welcome change.

I often found it ironic that there was little animosity here between Jew and Samaritan. We would discuss and argue about our differences, of course, but in the end it did not matter. Whether Jew or Samaritan, no matter how much we argued, we were all outcasts. All lepers. United in our disease. No other differences mattered. People who, in an ordinary life, would not associate with me, became the nearest thing to my friends that I had. Strange. There had been a time when I had despised every Jew, but now Simeon was my closest friend.

By the end of the week a band of them had decided to seek out this Jesus. I, too, wanted to go. Anything that could take my mind off my beloved family, whose lives were going on without me, was a welcome diversion. So it was agreed – I would join them. There would be ten of us. I was friends with a few of them, but some I knew hardly at all. We set off soon after we had decided to go. We moved slowly, for three of them had the disease in their legs and stumbled often. We headed north, through Samaria.

We got lucky at the first town we came to. We dared not go within the city gates, but spent some time begging for food outside. A woman took pity on us and baked us bread, leaving it a small distance away. The others did not acknowledge her, but shuffled forwards, heads down, to collect it. Many of the lepers were bitter about the way the world had forgotten and rejected us. But I was new enough to begging to appreciate any small act of kindness. I called out my thanks. The woman turned, surprised. She kept her distance but gave a small nod.

"Keep heading north," she advised. "He must be barely a day or two away." She started to move off, but I called out again.

"What? Who? Who do you speak of?"

"Jesus, of course. Why else would you be on the road but for hope that he might help you? He's travelling to Jerusalem. He will come on this road. Didn't you know?"

I shook my head in wonder. This was good news. I had been worried about entering Galilee. Now it seemed that we might not have to. I turned to the others, who were dividing up the bread.

"Did you hear that?" Some of them hadn't. There might be a new unity amongst us - between Jew and Samaritan - but there was no desire to engage between the sick and the healthy. Let alone a healthy Samaritan woman! I repeated her words in excitement.

"Perhaps God is with us," I finished.

Ashapod, a particularly bitter man at the best of times, shook his head. "Who knows?" he muttered. "But what can this Jesus actually do for us?"

None of us could answer that. We dared not voice our deepest, impossible hopes. But Joseph, a devout Jew, answered. "The weight of the sin that caused this bears heavily on me. I don't know what that sin was, but I see it in every diseased limb of mine. If he is a prophet from God, then perhaps he can lift this judgement. I bitterly regret not approaching John, the Baptist, two years ago by the Jordan. There were too many people there. To ask to go into the same waters as the healthy? They would never have allowed it. God in his mercy has given me a second chance, for a second prophet is here now. I won't waste this chance too. Even if he cannot change the sickness itself, to be rid of the judgement would be a miracle in itself."

Ashapod grunted, but I could see what Joseph said. To be rid of this shame – that would be a miracle in itself.

So slowly we moved north. We slept one night by the road, but moved off at the first stirrings of dawn. I continued to hope that we would meet him on the road – I didn't want to enter a town. I didn't want to see crowds of healthy people or happy families. I didn't want them to see me.

But by the end of the day we saw many people. The road became busy with people travelling south to Jerusalem. It was nearing the time of the feasts, and many would make the pilgrimage, wanting to arrive in plenty of time. They gave us a wide berth, and we tried to step to the side of the path. We kept crying out that we were lepers, as we were required to, whenever a new group approached. By now we were near the border of Samaria, where Galilee began. Further movement was impossible. The road had become crowded, and we were not allowed near people. We were by a village, so we stood a small distance from the entrance gates in a rocky patch under some trees to the side of the road, and all we could do was watch.

Ashapod depressed us with his grumblings. "Useless," he complained. "This is useless. How will we even see this miracle worker amid so many people? He won't want to come near us anyway."

Titus nodded in agreement. He sat on a rock – he was one whose legs were bad. He was glad to rest. But Reuben, a younger man, spoke up.

"It's not useless. It's our only hope. And it's good to be out of the village for a while, anyway." He paused, and a note of despair crept into his voice as he whispered, "I don't want to go back."

Joseph looked across. "Come, Reuben, stand with me. Let's see if we can find news of this Jesus." Reuben was the least disfigured of us, so it made sense for him to stand near the front of us and call to people.

"Jesus!" he shouted. "Is there news of Jesus?"

Most people ignored him, but eventually an old man replied. "He's not far back. With the fishermen. A few minutes away."

My heart leapt. No matter how much I told myself a cure was impossible, a wild hope would not be suppressed. We all stood now. Not daring to edge forward, but watching the crowds of townspeople pass. Minutes later, we saw within the crowd some larger, rougher looking men. They had to be the fishermen from Galilee. Jesus must be there. Now we all cried out, "Jesus, Master, have mercy on us!"

The movement halted. A stillness descended and a man emerged from behind the larger fisherman. He looked small beside them, and yet, something about him seemed large, too. He was not handsome, or striking; at first glance he looked, well, ordinary. But there was something about him that commanded attention. He took steps towards us, and stopped. There was a hiss in the crowds, an intake of many breaths. I could hear people muttering the word, 'Lepers!' I could see a woman on the edge of my vision pulling her curious child back. We were a sorry sight, really. Faces turned away. We displayed the disease that no one wanted. To look at us would be a reminder of what could happen to any one of them. It was fearful. I couldn't blame them for looking away. My hand automatically flew up to cover the patch I knew was on my cheek. I looked down at the dusty earth, very aware of Jesus who stood unmoving, not far from us. I had to risk it. I glanced up and was caught in his gaze.

Jesus was looking at us. Sometimes people did. It was rare - most preferred to look away. But some would look, and some might stare. Some would look in morbid fascination to see our disfigured faces. Others viewed us with disgust. Still others would look with helpless pity, or study us with a kind of professional interest. All of these looks were hard to meet. The shame I would feel was overwhelming when people looked at me – and I was far less disfigured than some. But Jesus had none of these expressions on his face.

He looked at us suddenly - with compassion, yes - but also with something more. What was that expression? With a shock, I realised that he was looking at us with love. It seemed to me that his gaze was specifically on me, but when we spoke together later I found that we had all felt that. I knew that he knew what I was – a leper. He knew how I felt about it. He knew the sin that had brought me here, yet still he looked with love. Slowly I dropped my hand away from the patch on my face – the patch I had considered trying to rip away with my fingers before now. Still he looked at me with absolute acceptance and love. Then he spoke.

I don't know what I expected him to say. In my wildest of dreams, "Be healed", perhaps. Or maybe I expected him to pray over us, or to challenge us about our sins. But no. His words were staggeringly simple. "Go show yourselves to the priests."

Ashapod audibly gasped, but to my surprise he didn't say a word. We looked at each other. To go to the very priests who had confirmed our illness in the first place would be ridiculous. Once a leper, always a leper. The only point of seeing a priest would be if the disease had gone and we stood a chance of being declared clean. But Jesus' voice carried such an air of authority that we didn't stop to protest. Joseph nodded and we set off towards the village gates, towards the priest who would be in the village.

I was next to Titus, and noticed with a jolt that he was not stumbling or shuffling along on his bad legs, but moved as swiftly and confidently as Reuben did. "Titus!" I exclaimed. "Your legs!"

He stared at me in shocked wonder and promptly sat down, right there in the street, and hastily unwrapped the bandages around his legs. They dropped to the ground, never to be retrieved. Pale, unblemished skin lay underneath. My hand flew to the familiar rough patch on my cheek, only to find smooth skin there. I looked around. Joseph? Where was Joseph, with his twisted nose and missing teeth? Joseph was staring at us, looking years longer. His teeth were all there and his nose as hooked, but as straight, as any other Jew.

"He's done it!" I whispered. "We're healed!" We were within the city gates by now, but had not gone far.

"Come on! Let's go to the priest, as he told us. At last the cleansing rites of Leviticus 14 can be used!" It was Ashapod who urged us, sounding shocked but happy. I had never heard him speak like that before! He was right! Time after time, priests had followed the law of Leviticus 13 in dealing with the treatment of the disease, but how many had ever had cause to turn to the next

106

chapter to deal with the ceremonial cleansing? Titus leapt up and started to lead the way.

I hesitated. I felt dazed. Such a burden had been lifted from me. Healed! My heart gave a jolt as I realised I could return home. I could be with my family. Strength had returned already. I felt vibrant and alive. And there was no shame. It had fallen away as surely as Titus's bandages, never to be picked up again. I was not just healed – I was restored. No longer a leper, now I could be a builder again. I was a Samaritan, a husband, a father, a man. All because of Jesus.

"Amon!?" It was Joseph. "Are you coming?"

It was all because of Jesus. I was close to tears with the sheer power of my gratitude. I glanced back up the hill. Some of the people had started to move. No one approached us – they weren't as sure as we were of our healing yet. Just fifteen minutes ago I would never have dared to get anywhere close to that crowd. But now I caught a glimpse of Jesus' robe and, ignoring Joseph's call, I ran back up the hill. Oh the joy of running, of not having to worry about stumbling, of tingling or numbed feet! As I ran my heart pounded and I threw back my head, crying, "Praise the Lord God!" I knew that such a miracle had not come from man, but from the Lord Almighty.

People made way for me. There were more Jews than Samaritans here, though we were on the border. I supposed that many of these Jews were travelling with Jesus. They wouldn't want to associate with a Samaritan. Not with someone so recently unclean, who hadn't yet been formally proclaimed clean by the priest, even though it was obvious to all by now that healing had occurred. To them I might be healed, but I was not yet clean. I

107

was still unacceptable by the sheer fact of my beliefs. I passed easily through them and threw myself onto the ground in front of Jesus. My face was wet with tears of gratitude. Out of breath now, I gasped out my inadequate thanks.

He knelt, grasped my hands, looked into my eyes and smiled. For a second I felt I could look into his soul, and I saw pure goodness. Still holding me, he looked around at the people and asked a question. "Didn't I heal ten men? Where are the other nine? Has no one returned to give glory to God except this..." and his grasp tightened, "...foreigner?"

I knew the word was not used in insult. These Jews thought themselves superior by virtue of their beliefs alone. Yet it was only I - a non-Jew - who had returned to give thanks. To him, a Samaritan was not to be shunned. The label didn't matter. The fact that my heart gave thanks to God mattered greatly. His touch remained on me. Warm and accepting hands grasped mine. What it felt to be touched by another after all this time was indescribable. My hands were held and steadied by this man who had released such healing upon me. He stood, pulling me to my feet, and smiled at me again. His voice was warm. "Stand up and go. Your faith has healed you."

Never again would I argue with a Jew about which of us was right. Jesus was as Jewish as any of them. He had brought my healing, yet had not even questioned my beliefs. He said my faith had healed me. Love for God - who I knew now was a God of Love - flooded my being. As he urged me to go, a vision of my wife came to mind. I started to thank him one last time, and now laughing he pushed me on the shoulder. "Go!!" And I went. Running at first, running through the crowd of those heading south, back into

108

Samaria, until I could run no more. Back home. Soon I would be there. Soon I would swing my sons over my head. I would hold Deborah and kiss my wife. Shame had been banished from our household, and would never return.

I would never have to return to the leper village. Yet even as I thought that, I thought of Simeon. I would send word. I would send food. I would never ignore or shun a leper again. Now I would be in a position to help them. I wished for a second that Jesus himself would come with me, and heal them all. He could do it. He could heal the entire world. I had no doubt that he could heal the whole world from this day, right until the end of time. But I had no idea how he would do it....

Meditation

No cause is too hopeless, or too hard for Jesus. Do you need healing? He heals on more than one level – physically and emotionally.

He can deliver us from all sorts of evil. No matter where we have been, he is never ashamed of us. He removes every bit of shame and makes all things new. Rescuing people is something he delights in.

Poem - Forgiven

I had stolen something precious and wrecked it.
It was not mine to destroy – but I destroyed it.
I hurt others, I hurt me, and I was the guilty one.

Can you imagine how I felt?

I knew it was all my fault. Everyone knew it. The priests knew it.
They came for me.....I knew the punishment was death.
They would hurl stones at me until I was dead.

Can you imagine how I felt?
Guilty. Shamed. Scared.

They took me to some new preacher.
They told him I had been caught red-handed....
'Shall we kill her?' they asked.
He didn't meet my eye...he looked at the floor and drew squiggles
in the sand.
I looked down too.

Can you imagine how I felt?
Guilty. Shamed. Scared.

And then he looked at those gathered before him and said,
"Who here has ever done no wrong, he can throw the first stone."
Silence fell. A puzzled silence. Then I heard the shuffle of feet....
The guilty tread of many feet leaving, until there was just me and
him left.

Can you imagine how I felt?
Shocked. Disbelief. Hope.

It grew silent. I dared to look at him.
And then... he looked... at me. Into me.

His eyes...love and compassion in his eyes.
" I will not condemn you either," he said.
"Now go, and change your ways......"

Can you imagine how I felt?
Forgiven. Cleansed. In love.

Can you imagine how I feel?
Forgiven. Cleansed. In love.

Zacchaeus' Story

I lived next door to him, and I wished I didn't. He was a miserable, unpleasant neighbour to have. You know the type – he never greeted us like other people did – with a hearty 'good morning'. No, not Zacchaeus. He barely looked up. He just shuffled out of his house with his head down. It would have been hard to know if he ever smiled, for his bushy beard completely hid his mouth.

He was already living there when I moved in. I inherited the house in the hot, dusty streets of Jericho when my uncle died. My uncle was unmarried. He had been estranged from my father, so I never really knew him. He had not come to my father's funeral. But word reached me that he was ailing, so I made my way to Jericho, sending word ahead. I arrived too late, yet I was surprised to find all his possessions - including his house and his olive groves - were my inheritance. So, like his olive trees, which were now my olive trees, I sunk my roots into the soil of Jericho. It was more fertile than my father's lands, which I sold, and I soon became prosperous.

The bane of every prosperous man, however, were the taxes that the Romans extorted from us. Taxes in Jericho were high – it was an important centre for the collection of the Roman tribute due to its situation. The tax collectors were both vigilant and dishonest. Crooks, all of them, taking more than was necessary or just. Even the Pharisees – not always noted for their honesty – denounced them. They were banned from the synagogue. They were proclaimed unclean. But it didn't stop them. They didn't even care about religion. They only cared about extorting money. And the worst of them was Zacchaeus. My neighbour, Zacchaeus.

112

Who knows what drew him to such an abhorrent 'profession'? Surely no God-fearing Jew would serve our oppressors with such zeal? I had heard stories and rumours about how such a situation came about, of course. Everything was blamed, from bad family blood to unrequited love. It was hard to know what to believe. Perhaps the most reliable of rumours came from Haral. Haral, now a merchant and a good friend of mine, had been brought up in the poorer streets where, it was rumoured, Zacchaeus had his origins too. Haral spoke about the boy Zacchaeus. Zacchaeus had always been on the small side, so he said. The lad had been mercilessly teased. Perhaps his size made him an easy target. If the bigger boys picked a fight, he dared not fight back. But then things started to happen to those bigger boys. Zacchaeus would tell tales - subtle half truths - about them to the Rabbi. Even tales about their families. A boy called Jacob once gave Zacchaeus a beating, so the story went. The next thing Jacob knew was that stories started to circulate about his older sister. The Pharisees went to see the family – what was the girl doing, wandering around in the evening with no head covering? Jacob's parents and his sister all denied it, of course. But rumours have a way of besmirching a family. The families - who had been wondering about whether the girl would be a good match for their sons - withdrew and looked elsewhere. The girl was disgraced. No one put it down to Zacchaeus's doing at the time – he was just a lad. But then similar stories started to circulate about others who had picked on him. Or wild goats were found in the morning in their family's crop fields. Little things, hard to prove, but eventually people began to connect the bad things that happened to the growing boy named Zacchaeus. Parents told their children to leave him alone. At some point in his life Zacchaeus had got in with the Roman authorities – no one seemed to know how or why. The friendless loner that he was by now found a degree of acceptance by the Romans, as long as he was useful to them. As a man, he became one of their tax collectors. He was successful, and became rich. He brought in more than any others, for the authorities as well as his own pocket. Before long the Romans made him the chief tax collector. He remained friendless but became very, very wealthy, living off the fruit of his neighbours' hard work.

Haral said that, as a boy, Zacchaeus had sometimes looked scared or cowed, like a perennial victim, but that there had also been slyness in his face. As he aged and became a loner, an aloof expression grew there. He seemed to squint a lot of the time, and never looked a person in the eye. Then he grew the beard, and took to wearing hats. His face was almost hidden, and few wanted to really look at him anyway. I rather fancied myself as an artist at times, but had you asked me to sketch his likeness, I would have struggled. I would draw a little Jew, recognisable only by his hunched shoulders and his short stature. His face would be almost featureless, hidden in shadow between the hat and the beard, for like so many others I had barely ever looked at the man. His eyes would be as I had only ever seen them – little half closed slits, looking slyly to one side.

Any rumours about Zacchaeus these days were only whispered, for he seemed to have ears everywhere, and I soon learned that it was unwise to make a public enemy of the man. Anyone who openly complained about him or mocked him found their taxes increasing beyond any reasonable amount. He wielded power. For whilst he undoubtedly creamed off an unhealthy amount of our money for himself, more than was legally necessary also found its way into the Roman coffers. Which meant he had

influence - and no one wanted a Roman soldier at their door. No –
it was unwise to publicly slight Zacchaeus, but there were subtle
ways of shunning such a man. You could turn your back as he
approached. You could simply pay your taxes as late as you dared
- silently, with no word spoken to the man. Most wealthy Jews
refused to even pay them in person but preferred to trust an
honest messenger or servant – all of whom also regarded such a
pawn of the Romans with as much disdain as they dared.

Finding myself living next door to such a man was one of the few
things I disliked about my new situation. It was impossible to hide
the extent of my new wealth from such a vigilant neighbour.
Moving was out of the question, for who would willingly buy a
house next door to the chief tax collector? True - our houses in
this part of the town were bigger than those elsewhere, but they
were still close. Privacy was hard to find. True - the rooms of our
houses surrounded a private courtyard. Bur mine was not so
private. I did not need all the rooms I owned, and so I shared my
home with Caleb, the overseer who looked after my olive groves.
He was married, and lived there with his wife and four children.
The arrangement suited me – he was less likely to leave as his job
included his living arrangements. I trusted him. It also gave me
the freedom to travel on long trips from time to time, knowing
that my house and business were in safe hands. But it meant that
quiet privacy was hard to find – the courtyard was often occupied
by Caleb's children. Long ago I embraced the growing trend of
using one of the flat roofs as a refuge. It had the advantage of
catching what few breezes were around. I rarely used it in the
heat of the day, though I had had palms moved up there to
provide shade. In the evening, however, it was a pleasant place to
sit. But Zacchaeus could easily see the comings and goings of my

servants and of the traders. Perhaps some of them informed on me, for he had an uncanny knack of knowing how successful my crops had been. It was as if he had eyes on my very ledgers, and he demanded much more than was fair. I had no choice but to pay up, though I resented it. I was powerless to object. He was in with the Romans, and they had been known to seize the lands of those who refused to pay the taxes. So I paid, and I joined the ranks of those who turned their backs when Zacchaeus approached, and whispered unkind words about him as we lingered by the town gates.

Jericho was a major route through the nation. Many passed through it and the town was often rife with all sorts of rumours – they seemed to wash over the town in waves. From the rumours of uprisings, near and distant, to rumours of new prophets - everything was discussed alongside the town walls, where the men often gathered. Every morsel of gossip or information would be chewed over. Few believed the rumours that any of these so-called 'prophets' were significant, for it was hundreds of years since a real prophet had visited the nation. And yet... The rumours had increased. First there were persistent stories about a wild man named John, who some called the Baptist and others called Elijah. At that time he was preaching not far away in the wilderness of Judea. He attracted quite a crowd, and when those who had seen him passed through Jericho, we wanted to hear every word. They said he lived off wild locusts and honey and had even dared to denounce King Herod! Such stories were news indeed, yet they paled into near insignificance when the stories about Jesus started to reach our ears. Apparently Jesus was a friend or relation of John, but did far more than preach to wilderness crowds. He did more than baptise people. He performed miracles. He was some sort of healer, so they said. He taught in the synagogues, though he was not popular with the Pharisees for he questioned their teaching and their ways. Word was that Jesus even allowed women to travel with him. "Surely that discredits him entirely?" I argued, yet those who had seen him shook their heads. 'He has a strange way about him,' they said. They claimed that he was not good looking nor a man of stature, but had an 'air of authority' that silenced his critics. He had a way with words too, but of course, if he was healing cripples as they said – well, who could argue with that?

Then came the day - two months ago now - when he passed through Jericho. He had of course passed through Jericho before, but on each occasion I had been out of town, and he was less famous then. The last time he came, rumours of his power started to circulate. It was said that he had healed a blind man as he passed by. Now he was famous indeed, and everyone wanted a glimpse of him! The streets swelled in numbers. Not only with those who were following him or coming ahead of him, but every resident of Jericho seemed to have turned out. Such a buzz of anticipation. What would he do? Where would he go? Would he denounce our Pharisees? Heal our sick? Preach in our synagogue? Would he eat with the Rabbis and chiefs of the town? By now his fame had grown. People were curious. Occasionally the word 'Messiah' was whispered, triggering even more speculation and debate.

So we all turned out. I was there, along with a group of friends, neighbours and fellow traders. We had been waiting for an hour or so. Haral was there too, and it was he that nudged me – nodding his head in a backwards motion. I looked behind, but could see nothing.

"What?" I asked.

"Did you see him? Zacchaeus is back there."

I snorted. "What's he doing here?" I was surprised, though. You rarely saw Zacchaeus out and about, unless it was on business - busily shuffling between collecting taxes and visiting the Roman authorities.

"The same as the rest of us, I imagine," said Haral, sounding amused. "I don't rate his chances of getting a view, though – he's so short, and I'm not going to let him through."

I'm sure everyone around us felt the same. No one would dare to push Zacchaeus out of the way, but no one would let him through, either. Who did he think he was?

A movement seemed to pass through the crowd, and it became noisier. Was this Jesus approaching? Minutes passed. There were many strangers ahead of him on the road. It grew more tightly packed. Then a group of men – large, rough looking Galileans – appeared. Jesus was from Galilee, so rumour had it. They passed by just in front of us, and then I caught a glimpse of Jesus himself. He may have been from Galilee, but this was no burly fisherman. He was of a more slender build than his friends. 'Is this what all the fuss has been about?' I wondered, feeling momentarily let down. He wore a simple robe and looked – well - ordinary. And then his eyes scoured the crowd. They flickered over me, and I drew my breath in sharply. I felt oddly pierced, and both relived and disappointed when his eyes passed over me as if searching for someone else. Then he looked up. I followed his gaze and was overcome by a sudden desire to laugh. I smothered it and instead nudged Haral. He too looked up and caught his breath. There was

118

Zacchaeus, up in a sycamore tree of all places! In all his finery, too! Never had I seen such a ridiculous, undignified sight. And this from the snotty little Roman pawn who liked to think himself above all of us! It was an entertaining morning all right. We would laugh about this for weeks to come!

Yet it wasn't over. It was only just beginning. For Jesus had stopped now, with all his retinue. He stood looking up at the tree and, despite the noise – for people all around us were looking up at Zacchaeus now and nudging each other, muttering and chuckling – despite the noise his voice carried clearly. "Zacchaeus" - and I wondered how he knew his name – "Hurry – come down, for today I must stay at your house." There was a stunned silence. Had we heard that right? Yet Zacchaeus was clambering down the sycamore tree, looking flustered. His hat caught on a branch and tumbled into the road, but he didn't stop to pick it up. Hastily he made his way to Jesus. He passed nearby and I looked at his mean little face. It was red, and his eyes were wide open, almost protruding with surprise and delight. He was rubbing his hands, almost running now, as people parted to let him through. Jesus waited, a patient smile on his face. Ridiculous as it was, I suddenly found myself wishing that that smile was for me. Zacchaeus reached him and gingerly stretched out a hand to grasp the arm of Jesus. 'Master', he was saying... 'This way. This way...' and to everyone's amazement (even his friends looked surprised), Jesus went with him. The people who had lined the streets quickly formed into little groups. I heard the murmurs.

"Does he know Zacchaeus? He called him by name! Surely then, he must know what he does? How he cheats God's own people? Why would he go to his house?"

I glanced around and saw two of the town elders shaking their heads as they talked. Even they had been cheated by Zacchaeus. "Why would he go to the house of a sinner?" I could hear one of them saying in a deep grumble. But I stayed to hear no more. I was curious. I grabbed Haral's arm.

"Come on," I said. "Let's follow. This is the first time I've been glad that I live next door to the man."

Like everyone else I was taken aback that Jesus would visit someone like Zacchaeus, who was banned from associating with us good Jews. But then I thought, 'Perhaps Jesus will put him straight.' Yes, there could be some uncomfortable moments ahead for Zacchaeus as this Rabbi pointed out his wrongdoings. I expected that Jesus would just stay long enough to tear Zacchaeus off a strip. I expected a thoroughly sober and chastised Zacchaeus to emerge. That would be a sight!

"Come on!" I urged Haral again. It was odd, but no one else was following. The crowds stood in groups but neither followed nor dispersed. Once we were through them we hurried, reaching my street just in time to see Zacchaeus and Jesus entering Zacchaeus's house. Some of the Galileans were nearby. I wasn't sure if any of them had gone in as well.

Haral and I looked at each other. "Ah, well," I said. "Join me for some lunch."

We sat in the shade of the courtyard. Sometimes, when sitting there, you can hear neighbours if they too are outside. At first it was very quiet indeed. Zacchaeus and Jesus must have been inside. But then, gradually, we heard voices. The brogue of Galileans reached our curious ears. Then to our amazement we heard laughter. What did they have to laugh about? It went on and on. They must have gathered to eat outside. After a while it sounded like a party was in full flow. It must have continued for an hour or two. At last, however, the voices died down and we heard the sound of movement again, at which time we returned to the street. By now the crowd had re-gathered – not right outside Zacchaeus's house – for people were wary of him – but they waited in the street at the end of our short road.

Ahead of Jesus, a man emerged from the house. He had one of the happiest faces I had seen for a long time. His brown eyes shone out with joy, and he ran his fingers through his hatless, wavy hair. He could barely stand still, almost doing a jig on the spot. He was fairly short and – my goodness – I stared – it was Zacchaeus!!! He was wringing his hands with joy as he waited. Jesus followed him. He, too, looked full of joy, and he was laughing at Zacchaeus's obvious happiness. Amazing! No one ever laughed at Zacchaeus! And Zacchaeus never looked happy!

And now Zacchaeus looked around, and seemed to register the crowds for the first time. All eyes were on the little group. Zacchaeus laughed out loud and his voice boomed out. I had only ever heard him speak in a quiet, mean tone, but now his voice carried across the street and was full of joy.

He spoke, and initially his words were spoken to Jesus alone. He then, however, addressed us all.

"Lord, I will give half of my possessions to the poor." There was a collective gasp. Now Zacchaeus looked around the crowds. His gaze included everyone – even me, for that was where his eyes finally rested. "If I have defrauded anyone of anything, I will pay back four times as much". Though his voice was still loud and joyful, it was also serious. I had never trusted the man since the day I first saw him, but now I found myself believing every word.

People didn't know how to take it. They expressed delight, but underneath there was cynicism. Would Zacchaeus really keep his word once Jesus had left Jericho? Good intentions were all very well, but....

Jesus did not stay long after that. He passed on towards Jerusalem.

Despite his outburst, nobody knew quite what to expect from Zacchaeus in the following days and weeks. I expected him to take on an air of self-importance again. After all, Jesus – the famous Rabbi whom everyone had wanted to meet - had singled him out of the crowd and chosen to go to his house. I suspected that Zacchaeus would boast about that. I thought he might demand to be accepted into the synagogue. Perhaps he would want to take his place with us as we gathered by the town gates. Maybe he would pay back some, or even all, of what he had promised, but I suspected it would be done with an air of lording it over us. I thought his manner would express his self-importance even as he kept his promise to Jesus. I wondered what demands he would make upon us.

I could not have been more wrong. I wonder now if my suspicions say more about my own heart than anything else. I have hesitated to document all of this, expecting Zacchaeus's zeal to diminish and for him to revert to form. But his behaviour has been so different from what I expected, and he shows no sign of ever going back to the Zacchaeus we all knew – or thought we knew.

The day after Jesus visited, Zacchaeus started paying back all he had stolen. I was one of the first people he visited. I expected him to be shame-faced, if he kept his word at all. But there was none of it. His face was shining and he looked me in the eyes and grasped my hands, squeezing them tightly.

"To you, my neighbour, I come first. I've greatly wronged you. Not only by demanding more than the Romans needed, but also by snooping on you." At this he let out a snort and then bent over, convulsed with laughter and clutching his midriff helplessly. I stood rather stiffly, not seeing anything humorous about it. Eventually he straightened up, wiping tears of mirth from his eyes. He noticed my disapproval and once again took my arm.

"Ah, my friend and neighbour, forgive me. Allow me my joy, for it's been a lifetime coming. I've spent the night with my ledgers and with the very same servants who have helped me spy and keep account of you. And just as they let no wealth of yours go unmentioned, now they let not one denari I've stolen go unaccounted for. It's a wonderful kind of justice."

How could he be so open about his crimes? How could he laugh about them?

Still laughing quietly he clapped his hands and a servant – one of my own accountants, if you please – came out of his house bearing a small chest. The servant looked frightened – as well he might - for I would never allow him anywhere near my scrolls again. I could ruin the man if I publicly denounced him as a spy. Zacchaeus glanced at me and seemed to read my mind.

"Ah," he cajoled me, "Come now. I threatened the man. He had little choice but to spy on you, for I own the very house he lives in

123

and he has a large family who could not survive if I turned them out. Let this be a new day. In part it is due to him that you are now four times richer. For as I stole most from you – with his help – so you also stand to gain the most."

His logic bewildered me and, partly to hide my confusion, I bent to open the lid of the chest. It was indeed full of coins – some of them were gold. Zacchaeus stood chuckling before me, rubbing his hands and nodding, "It's all there, and more besides. It is good, yes? It is good?"

I stared at him. His face had changed. He now had such an open expression, like a delighted child. He had trimmed his beard. It was shorter, and the facial hair that usually hid his mouth was cut short. A generous smile beamed out. It was echoed in the twinkling brown eyes that regarded me. From the corners of his eyes, the lines that had once been a result of the hard and bitter years had been transformed into laughter lines.

I was aware that I had become like a statue before him and so I nodded stiffly. The whole thing was so strange that it was the most I could do. I still did not entirely trust this new Zacchaeus. I could not unbend to him, but perhaps I would not sack the deceitful servant hastily.

"Bring it in," I told the man tersely. He moved quickly to obey my order, still looking scared.

Zacchaeus beamed at me and had the audacity to call after the man, "You see! I told you he was a good man. He can be generous, too. He can be forgiving. He will keep you on, I'm sure"
I was dumbfounded. I had decided no such thing, but to sack the man now would make me appear even meaner than Zacchaeus

had been. I stared hard at Zacchaeus, trying to work out if he was being extremely cunning or just naive. But he didn't seem to be thinking about it at all.

"Well, well, my friend. I have many amends to make today, so I must be on my way. Yes, so much to pay back - it will take weeks." He sounded delighted about it. "The Romans will have to wait for their taxes now, for I'll be busy keeping my promise to Jesus." He laughed again, bowed and spun around, disappearing into his house. I stood there for some moments, replaying the strange encounter in my mind until, still shaking my head, I returned to my rooms.

And so it went on. Over the next few weeks Zacchaeus himself went to every household from whom he had previously collected taxes. Where he had once shuffled along the streets, keeping his head down, now he almost skipped along. He would stop to greet those whom he passed, his head held high and always laughing as he went, clutching his satchel full of money to be repaid. He had no shame about what he had done. I'd never seen a man so joyful.

He did none of the things I expected. He never attempted to join the town elders, or our group of merchants as we stood by the town walls. He didn't go near the synagogue. And he no longer frequented the Roman quarters where he used to be seen. No, instead he could now be found wandering around the poorer parts of the town. Rumour had it that, wherever he went, things started to change. He would be wandering around streets where the flat roofs were holed and damaged by the weather, and without a word to anyone, within days a group of workmen, paid in advance, would arrive to repair the roofs. He never boasted of this generosity, or even tell anyone that he had paid the men, but we knew from the workmen themselves that he was the benefactor.

A little later, I heard that cloth and sandals were being delivered to the poorer communities. Good cloth that would make clothes for adults and children alike. There were days when Zacchaeus 's servants would turn up there with donkeys loaded with bread or grain. Gradually people with needs would start to approach him in the streets, sometimes apologetically and, unlike even us more noble characters, he would never turn them away empty handed. He would never ignore a begger. Where we might perhaps toss them a coin, Zacchaeus might give them the same coin, but he would also stop and talk with them.

Some of those whom he had repaid started to call on him. I would see them from my rooftop. He would welcome anyone who called, ushering them happily into his courtyard. I could see him having food and drink brought out to them. There would be talk and laughter late into the night. Always I would hear Zacchaeus's delighted laugh ringing out the loudest. I couldn't bring myself to befriend him, but Haral would join these gatherings and tell me about them. Apparently Zacchaeus seemed to know many stories about Jesus. Whether the Galileans or Jesus himself had told him these things, or how he knew about them, no one seemed to know. Zacchaeus, however, loved to repeat these stories, and barely an evening went by without the Rabbi Jesus being mentioned.

Then came an evening – in fact it was just yesterday - when I glanced outside and noticed a beautiful sky. The sun was setting, the weather was warm and mellow, and I felt the call of the

126

outdoors. Occasionally I would stroll out through the gates to the town and walk among my olive groves. I also allowed others access to the land. But yesterday the groves were deserted and seemed to be full of a hazy peace. I just felt drawn there. I made my way to a small hillock which gave a good view of the setting sun. As I approached I heard soft humming and saw a figure sitting on a large boulder, also apparently watching the sinking sun. The air was warm and sweetly scented. It was the sort of atmosphere that made you feel well disposed to everyone, and even as I realised it was Zacchaeus who sat there, I did not withdraw, as I might have done had it been colder or had I felt differently.

I thought I made no sound as I stopped a little way back, yet his humming ceased and he called out without turning around.

"Is that my good neighbour? How kind you are to allow us to stroll through your groves. What a view there is from here."

I moved closer until I stood by him.

"Zacchaeus", I greeted him cautiously.

He glanced at me and smiled. "But you've come to walk in solitude, and here I am, stealing your view. I will leave you to your reverie." He made as if to move, but I raised my hand to stop him.

"No. Stay." I surprised myself with the words. I realised I desperately wanted to talk to him. I was curious, and I wanted some answers. It was rare to catch this 'loner' on his own these days. I tried to make myself sound less desperate, and added gruffly, "after all, it's not my view, although I own the land we stand on. The Lord created it."

He settled back down and nodded, chuckling. "Ah, the Lord. Yes. The Lord created the heavens and the earth. You know, I used to think that that was a such a hard and laborious work he performed. But now I know it was joy - a pure joy for Him to create it with such love."

The man baffled me. How long was it since he had been to a synagogue? How would he know such a thing?

I cleared my throat, wondering how to get to the heart of what I wanted to know. "Zacchaeus," I started. "I was not sure the change in you would last. But you've proved me wrong. I have to er... commend you for it."

"Ah. The change in me. Don't commend me, my friend. I've done nothing to change myself." He threw me a sharp sideways glance, startling me. For an instant it seemed to pierce me. "You're wondering how on earth Jesus brought about such a change?"

He had cut to the heart of what I had hardly dared to voice. "Um. Yes. We thought... I thought... what with the way things had been... why did he come to you? What did he say to cause such change?"

Zacchaeus was quiet for a long moment. When he spoke, it was not with laughter but with wonder in his voice. "Why did he come to me? I cannot say. I did nothing to earn such favour, God knows. As do you, of all people. But come he did, and it was nothing specific that he said. It was who he was. I've never met such a man." He paused for a long time, and then continued. "You thought – you all thought – that perhaps I was in for trouble. That he had come to rebuke me for my dishonest ways. I certainly would have deserved such a rebuke. We talked about many things which were for my ears alone, yet every word he spoke made me feel that he knew me through and through. With all my mean heart, dishonest ways and evil thoughts , he was still pleased to be there. He could see the very worst things about me, yet he was content to sit at my table and share my bread. To smile into my eyes with appreciation and love." Another long pause. "As we sat there, even in silence after a while, I could feel my heart warming up. It was like the sun coming up after a frost... a slow, thawing warmth which became hotter and hotter until it was ablaze and I had to laugh with joy lest I burst. Nothing else mattered. How he laughed with me. We were beyond the land of words. I only have to think of him and it's like the sun coming up all over again," He looked at me properly now, and his eyes seemed to glow as they reflected the sunset. He was beaming. "In that moment, nothing mattered except being there with him. The riches, any power I had – it all became meaningless and I care nothing for it now. There's nothing special about me, my friend. Anything special has to do with Him."

The sun disappeared below the horizon now, and the sky turned from orange to deeper red.

"It will be dark shortly," I said abruptly, changing the subject.

Zacchaeus stood up and stretched, nodding. "Yes. Shall we walk back together?"

I had hoped we could do that, but felt strangely awkward in suggesting such a thing. I was glad it came from him.

"Yes." I knew I still sounded stilted and awkward, even unfriendly. But Zacchaeus didn't seem to mind. He just smiled, nodded and chuckled, and we walked back through the olive groves in an amicable silence.

I cannot stop thinking about this Jesus. Had a crippled man lived next door, and had Jesus fixed his legs, I would have been impressed, but after the weeks had passed I would have got used to seeing the man walk and thought no more about it.

But he has done much more than this. He has, in the course of a few hours, completely transformed a man whom I thought I knew. A man I thought would never change has become a completely different person. From the inside out. I find myself hoping to become a friend of this man. A man whom I despised not long ago. A man whom everyone despised.

It's as if Zacchaeus has been loved into becoming a different person, and I can't help wondering if the same thing could happen to me....

It's strange. It used to be that when I looked at Zacchaeus I saw a small man. Whilst his stature is unchanged, it's as if he has grown more than any of us. I just don't think of him as small anymore. I see a man with a large heart, and it draws me to the one who caused this transformation. So I'm putting my olive groves completely into the hands of Caleb for now. I'm packing my bags and preparing to follow this man to Jerusalem. Soon it will be the Passover feast. Time for the lambs to be slaughtered and sacrificed in memory of the Lord God's great rescue plan for his people. I am hoping that Jesus will be there for the feast of the lambs that were slain.

Meditation

Imagine Jesus had picked you out of the crowd and said he wanted to visit you.
How would you feel?
What would you do?
Let the scene play out in your imagination. What would Jesus talk to you about? Is there anything you would say to him, or ask him about?
Don't forget – there is love in his eyes.
Would you change as a result of your time together? How?

Poem - Imagine

Imagine
picking uncouth fishermen to change the world
Imagine
sacking most of the army before a major battle
Imagine
crying as I gaze into your face of love
Imagine
your rescue plan for humanity depending on your willingness to
die
Imagine
a king dancing and leaping near-naked in the street
Imagine
telling a child to feed thousands with five loaves and two fish
Imagine
touching a leper
Imagine
A King taking tea with a man up a tree
Imagine
laughing and laughing and laughing even in your awesome
presence

How utterly foolish
How brilliantly wise

Martha's Story - Part 2 – Lazarus

After that first, extravagant meal I'd thrown for Jesus - when he'd had called me his dearest - he continued to visit us regularly. He made the trip to Jerusalem every year for the Passover, and other times besides. We were only two miles from the city, so he would sometimes come and eat or stay the night with us after being in the city by day. Sometimes all his friends would come too. At other times, just Peter and John and maybe one or two of the others would be with him.

What joy we had when they visited! John became a good friend to Lazarus, too. Soon after their arrival, after greetings and refreshments, Lazarus would ask, "So tell us your news..." and the stories would flow. Amazing, moving, almost unbelievable stories. Some of the things that happened! Peter would butt in loudly and tell us some of the startling things Jesus had been saying. I worried sometimes about the brushes he had with authority - they appeared to be happening with increasing intensity and regularity. A vitriolic hatred seemed to be growing in the hearts of the Pharisees and priests - who so often earned Jesus' harshest words. I wondered where it would lead. But the men were unstoppable and brashly confident in the power and person of Jesus – they knew no fear. And as they told us of miracles and healings I could see why. Jesus himself never spoke of his exploits. He was often weary when he arrived. He would recline - lying, like the others, on the floor mats. Mary would bring cushions for him to lean against and often he would doze off, even as his men were speaking of blind people healed or demons cast out. Once the latest stories of their public exploits had been shared, Peter too would often drop off. Perhaps our wine was too good! But when

Peter or James ran out of steam, John would pick up the narrative, often telling us of other moments, away from the crowds. I remember the day when he grew still and looked at us, eyes shining, and whispered, "He stilled a storm."

I didn't understand. I thought he was talking figuratively. "He has always been good at getting people to listen..." I started, but John shook his head emphatically.

"No. I mean – a storm. On Lake Galilee. A real storm. We were in the boat when a squall came from nowhere. We were taking on water, winds were howling and the sky was black. Even Peter was terrified. He woke Jesus."

Peter was there on that occasion, dozing nearby. His name must have penetrated his mind, for suddenly he stirred. He rubbed his eyes. "What? What's that?"

John smiled. "I was telling them about the storm. Martha didn't think I meant a real storm."

Peter sat up, fully awake now. He looked at me, his expression unusually serious. "Ah, yes. The storm. I've never been in such a sudden and evil wind. How it howled! It was like there were demons screaming all around us. No one dared wake Jesus at first, but I knew we had to. So I did."

"So what happened?" I asked impatiently.

Peter shook his large, shaggy head in wonder. "Just three words. He spoke just three words to the weather – after he had rebuked us for our lack of faith once again." He added this with a laugh, but grew serious again. "Peace. Be still." It was like a giant hand stopping a runaway cart halfway down a hill. The wind didn't die down. It stopped. An instant calm fell on the sea. The clouds simply vanished. It was evening, and the stars appeared as suddenly as they must have done when the Lord God spoke them into being. I've been on that lake since I was a child, and I've never seen anything like it!"

John spoke, pride in his voice. "It truly was the power of God." Peter nodded.

It was just one of many stories they told. By now, in my heart, I had long thought that Jesus was more than a prophet. He seemed to have a direct connection to heaven. I knew the stories of the power that Moses, Elijah, Elisha and others had wielded in the name of the Lord. They too performed wonders with the power of God. But Jesus seemed to do more than perform those amazing wonders from time to time. They happened all around him on a daily basis, it seemed. Wonders just spilled out of him. His very being was wondrous. I was convinced the earth had never before contained a man who walked so closely to God. I knew the stories of a coming Messiah, too. And I dared to believe that he had come. Why else would Jesus not only transform people and places with his power, but also challenge the authorities as he did? I watched and listened with a growing excitement in my heart.

When Jesus and his disciples had moved on, Mary and I would talk endlessly about all we had heard. Sometimes we would go into Jerusalem and visit our relatives there, to hear the stories they could tell. But still I preferred to hear them from the mouths of his closest friends.

Jesus had become famous. Was it really less than three years since we had first met him? How his fame had grown in that time!

It amazed me that he had not distanced himself from us. He could have taken his pick of many influential houses in the city now – many wealthy men would love to dine with him. Sometimes he did eat with them, but he still seemed to prefer our humble little house in Bethany. Even when he was teaching in the city, he would sometimes return to us in the evening, even staying the night in Bethany. It amazed me – and yet, knowing him as I did – it also did not surprise me. For he was a man who loved his friends and was faithful to them.

Then there was the day when I seriously wondered if I even knew him. The day when my trust faltered, and I wondered if he cared for us at all.

It hurts me to recall those few days. The swiftness of the fever that came upon our dear brother, Lazarus. One evening he went early to rest, complaining of stomach pains and a headache. The following morning he couldn't rise. We hoped the fever would pass swiftly as we treated him with herbs. But soon I sent Abdown - a servant - to Jerusalem to fetch a good doctor. The doctor looked worried. That scared me. Mary tugged at my arm, repeating the advice she had been giving since that morning.

"Martha – we should send for Jesus. We've heard he's not far away. He's probably coming here anyway. He'll be able to help." This time I didn't shrug her off by telling her that our brother would recover before Jesus even arrived. I saw the grave expression on the face of the physician and I was frightened. Slowly I nodded. "Yes, I believe he will. He will come. He cares for Lazarus as if he were his own brother."

I hadn't wanted to interrupt the work of Jesus, but there was too much at stake now. Even so, I didn't want him to feel ordered around by a woman. I didn't want his reputation to suffer, though he himself seemed to care little about what others thought. I knew he would come. I knew he would heal Lazarus. In the end I called Abdown again. "Go to Jesus. He shouldn't be hard to find. He's somewhere on the road beyond Jerusalem. People will know where he is. Give him this message: 'Lord, your dear friend is very sick'. That's enough. He will see you and know who sent you. He will come."

He left at a run. It was evening, and he had returned the following day, well before noon. He had returned alone. I was not concerned at first – I had not expected Jesus to run! But Abdown said that Jesus had sent no message back. No indication of when he would arrive. I questioned him man closely. Lazarus was now far worse – barely conscious.

"But did he move at all? Did he appear to be taking his leave of people?"

Abdown looked down and shrugged. He would not meet my eyes. I feared he was close to the tears that I myself felt gathering, somewhere deep inside. I dismissed him at last. Surely Jesus would come?

It was such an anxious day. I have dreadful memories of Mary crouched over Lazarus, tending to him, whispering to him that Jesus was coming. To just hold on, for Jesus was coming. But Lazarus did not hold on. In the afternoon he slipped into a coma. His face was white. There were the dark rings under his eyes. Even they paled as time ticked by and he took on a waxy complexion. There were no last words; no goodbyes. He just went. In the early hours of the following morning while it was still

137

dark. Mary and I clutched at each other in disbelief – too shocked to even cry. Where was Jesus?

I stumbled into the kitchen, heading for the storeroom beyond, and came to an abrupt halt. Abdown or perhaps Dara had left a pile of linen and a large jar of ointment out on the floor, by a small lamp. The smell of the aromatic spices hit me as soon as I walked in. I vaguely remembered my loyal servant suggesting preparations like this some hours earlier. I had sent her away in anger. Such preparations were for the dead.

"No," I had said in a harsh whisper. "Jesus has been summoned. We won't need such things."

I had been wrong, and now I was grateful to the girl. I heard something. A whimper. I picked up the lamp and moved around the small room. I found Dara sitting in a corner. She almost cringed as I approached, as if expecting more of my anger. My mouth twitched as I tried to smile, but it disobediently twisted itself into an expression of grief. I swallowed hard and beckoned the girl. She stood, reading the events in my face, and her tears spilt over. I nodded. "It's over. Will you help us prepare him?"

It was my way of thanking her and of making amends for my earlier harshness. I had intended to do all the necessary work with Mary. Dara nodded – she too had loved our brother. He was a gentle soul. Not well known in the town, but loved by those who knew him.

I picked up the linen, noticing the plain shift on top. Dara took the jug and a wide bowl and followed me back into his room. She then went back outside for water. Mary and I washed the body of our brother while Dara started to tear the linen into strips before soaking them, one by one, in the ointment. Every time I heard a loud tear in the cloth it felt as if another piece of my heart was being torn up. I gently lifted Lazarus's head and Mary clothed him in the slip. Together we bound him with the strips of linen. It was a relief to be able to do something at last, and yet it wasn't – it was a living nightmare. I kept expecting him to open his eyes and declare that it was all a bad joke. The hardest thing was to wrap his dear head in the final large piece of linen. To know that those large brown eyes, usually serious but sometimes full of mischief, would never open again. It was starting to sink in. Mary and I sat kneeling on our heels as Dara quietly took the empty jug, the bowl, and the remaining few rags, and slipped out of the room. Suddenly Mary moved, reaching for me blindly. She lurched into me, and we held onto each other as if drowning. Her body was racked with sobs, silent ones at first, but becoming ever louder until they released mine. We wept together, as broken as we had ever been.

There were still hours before dawn, and neither of us had slept these last few days.

"Mary, we should rest." I urged her to our room. Our hands reeked of the spices, but I knew the scent would not easily leave now. There was no point in washing. The whole house was impregnated with this smell of death. I lay beside Mary and held her. Exhaustion won her over, but my own mind was too active to give in to sleep.

I lay awake, fretting. Where was Jesus? Abdown was trusted and loyal. Surely he could not have got the message wrong, or lied about delivering it? I had questioned him twice more that evening about Jesus' exact response. I had been so harsh with him that in

139

the end he had broken down, weeping. He too loved our brother. My mind kept turning over the questions and the situation, trying to make sense of it. Jesus knew Lazarus was sick. Jesus loved Lazarus – he loved all of us. Jesus was a man in demand these days. Jesus had the power to heal Lazarus. Jesus would put his friends above his ministry. Jesus was scathing towards the Pharisees who made their religion more important than helping people. So surely Jesus would drop everything and come? But Jesus was not here. Had something happened? Something to prevent him from coming? Could he be sick, too? Maybe the crowds wouldn't let him pass? But he had power. Where was he?

I couldn't rest. My mind wrestled with the questions until they subsided, unanswered, as they were overtaken by the realisation that tomorrow – no, today – we would have to bury my brother. There were arrangements to be made. It was a relief to think about that instead. At least there were things I could do there. My questions would have to wait until I saw Jesus at the burial.

I rose as early as was decent. I tried to rise without disturbing my sister, but she stirred as I moved. Her drowsy eyes, still red rimmed and exhausted, stared at me in desolation.

"I'll wake the servants - we must send out the news," I said. "He must be buried today."

Soon our house was filling up. Our nearby cousins arrived first, with our aunt and uncle. Then our other cousins from Jerusalem came. Friends of Lazarus arrived, along with the priest. Neighbours assembled. Old family friends gathered. The body of our brother was put gently on to the bier and lifted by the men. Soon we were on our way to the tombs. It had all happened so fast. I felt like I was playing a part in a bad dream.

Still my eyes strayed to the road from Jerusalem as I walked near the front of the procession. Surely Jesus had had more than enough time to reach us by now? Abdown had been back a whole day. I couldn't believe that Jesus would intentionally miss the burial. But still he did not arrive. The noise of people wailing at the tomb hurt my head – my tears had dried up once people started to arrive. Mary stood tearfully by my side. We both wore heavy, uncomfortable robes and walked barefoot as a sign of our grief.

What can be said? He was buried - laid gently on the floor of the tomb. Laid to rest while those who loved him found no rest. We stayed by the tomb. The house was unclean now – it would have to be purified. Even the priest left hastily, afraid that perhaps he would be tainted.

So we grieved. Our family stayed. They would remain with us for the entire seven days of mourning. I supposed we would then have a feast as was the custom, but for now we fasted. Fancy! Me, Martha, completely disinterested in preparing a feast. I was renowned for my kitchen, but now I cared nothing for it. The sharp acid of loss ate away at my heart, and above all, around all our combined grief, was the question: 'Where was Jesus?' We had boasted of his friendship. We had claimed that here was a man who showed us what the love of God was like. Yet we were the very ones he had abandoned in our moment of greatest need. It was unfathomable. At first our relatives and friends were too kind to say much about it, but after three days I heard his name muttered with increasingly frequency.

"Wasn't Jesus a close family friend? Is he coming for the feast?"

"I don't know. I don't know why he wasn't here for the burial. He isn't far, so they say, and he was summoned."

I refused to answer such comments, but at night, in our room, I would speak with Mary about it.

"I hope he comes for the feast. I wish he'd been here for the burial. But even more than that, why didn't he come when something could be done for Lazarus?"

Mary was gazing out of the window, though it was dark and cloudy and there was nothing to be seen. Her voice was soft as she repeated the phrase that was on our lips every time we discussed Jesus and his whereabouts these last days, "If he had been here...."

Mary turned to me. Her face was wet again. "Martha," she said softly, "I still love him."

I nodded sadly. "I think I do too, Mary, though I confess there have been moments these last days when it has felt more like hate. Were he to appear here, right now, I might be angry with him. But I would still love him. I think perhaps I might even trust him. But I don't understand him.

I lay down on my bed and we grew silent. Mary still sat at the window.

As usual the light woke me. The freshness of morning greeted me through the window, and I nearly smiled at it until I remembered that my brother was dead. I think it was the first unbroken night's sleep I had had in a week – was it only a week since all this started? I rose, and the weight of my grief made my heavy, mourning robes feel light. Another day. I was grateful for the love and comfort expressed by my relatives, but the one person I wished for was not here. Part of me wanted everyone to go so that I could really consider this and make some sort of sense of it. I still felt as if I were moving slowly through someone else's bad dream.

The day started in much the same way as the previous two days . The servants fetched water from the well to fill the water jars, and Dara milked the goat. Despite having slept, I still felt weary. We wandered outside and I sat in the shade of the house, gazing into the distance with a vacant mind.

By mid morning it was hot even in the shade. Young Sara sat talking by my side and kept trying - without success - to cheer me up. I let my young cousin chatter on, and her voice blended in with the birds overhead and the swish of the breeze in the fig trees. I wasn't listening to her. I noticed a dot on the horizon and idly concluded that it was a person, getting nearer all the time. As he drew closer, I noticed he was walking as quickly as the heat allowed. He was agitated, I surmised. He looked familiar. It was one of Jesus's friends. Andrew – it looked like Andrew. I rose abruptly, startling Sara into silence, and I set off towards Andrew. I reached him within minutes with both of us hurrying, and I searched his face. He looked a bit embarrassed but nodded in answer to my unspoken question. "Jesus is on his way. I came ahead to tell you. He is not ten minutes behind me."

"What held you up?" was my urgent question.

He would not meet my eyes, but turned to watch a child playing on the side of the street. "Jesus said we were to wait."

I stared at him. Why would Jesus say such a thing? But I knew Andrew had no answers. Without another word I headed on down the road. I saw a large dust cloud in the hazy heat ahead – it had to be Jesus and the rest of them. I caught up with them just outside the village. Jesus waved his friends onwards, allowing us a moment of privacy. Anger started to rise up in me, just as I had expressed to Mary the night before. But, as I looked at him, it died away. He met my eyes without hesitating. There was no embarrassment or shame in his eyes. He looked sad, as if he had suffered, or was he simply mirroring my own expression? There was compassion in his eyes, and I was undone by it.

"Lord," I started. He was my Lord, though I did not understand him. "If only you had been here..." That 'if only' that Mary and I had uttered daily... "my brother would not have died." I had said it. It was partly an accusation but also a question. Yet as I looked into the face of love, I realised that, yes, I still trusted him. I wanted him to know. So I blurted out, "But even now I know God will give you whatever you ask."

Jesus nodded and added the words that I would have loved to have heard the moment my brother ceased to breathe. "Your brother will rise again." It was a statement of certainty. I had long since dismissed the Sadducees' teaching that there was no resurrection. It did not fit with what Jesus promised. Even the Pharisees agreed with him on that one.

"Yes," I said, "He will rise when everyone rises, at the last day."

Jesus spoke to me again, and his words had an authority about them. He spoke directly to my heart, and yet it seemed like he also spoke to the air, to the birds, to the trees and to every unseen spirit. "I am the resurrection and the life. Anyone who

144

believes in me will live, even after dying. Everyone who lives in me and believes in me will never die." There was such an intensity about him. "Do you believe this, Martha?"

I did not wholly understand all his words, but I knew what he was asking me.

It was no longer about Lazarus. Lazarus was safe. This was about Jesus, and who he was. It was about whether I trusted him. I spoke in a clearer voice than I had used for days. I spoke like someone waking up after a long sleep. I spoke like someone not in a dream, but awake and alive.

"Yes, Lord. I have always believed you are the Messiah, the Son of God, the one who has come into the world from God." We looked at each other, and I could feel his pleasure. Mary crossed my mind. Mary! She too would want to speak to him. And alone would be better. There were too many people at the house. I looked at him and, without a word passing between us, I knew he would wait there. I turned and hurried to the house.

"Mary!" I called whilst some way off. People looked up, startled, but I only had eyes for Mary who was sitting close by a couple of people near the house. She had been crying again – her eyes were red. She came to me and I lowered my voice. "Jesus is waiting for you, just outside the village." The words were barely out of my mouth before she flew past in unseemly haste – though I didn't care about that. I understood, even if no one else did. Others were curious, though, and they joined me in following Mary. "She must be going to the tomb," someone said. Anna and Maria were both crying – I assumed they were the ones I had seen with Mary by the house.

Mary told me later that she had greeted Jesus with the very same words that I had used. "If only you had been here my brother would not have died." She could say no more, she was sobbing so hard. Jesus had not spoken to her about resurrection, or challenged her trust - perhaps he didn't need to. He simply asked where Lazarus was, and made his way with her to the tomb.

I caught up with them by the time he arrived. There were a lot of people there. Everyone had followed us from the house, and a crowd must have followed Jesus from Jerusalem as he passed. His friends, yes, and possibly even some of his critics – they watched his every move in and around Jerusalem. Mary was completely distraught. Anna and Maria had also caught up and sat, either side of her, on the ground near Jesus. Mary's head was in Anna's lap. She sobbed with raw grief and Anna too, wept, as did Maria on her other side. I felt my own tears start to run again. Jesus' gaze went from me to the group of the three women in the dirt and across the crowd. I followed it and could see others in the crowd also weeping. These were not the false tears of professional mourners. Here were Lazarus's friends and family, weeping at the way his precious life had been torn away from them. The separation between life and death was tangible and final. We stood, looking at the grave, along with Jesus - a man who was more alive that anyone I ever knew. The man who seemed to me to be 'Life' personified stood, looking at death and the anguish it caused, and then he too started to weep.

The sound was shocking. I will never forget the sound of his raw pain. He didn't cover his face with his hands, he just sobbed. His body shook with grief.

People stared. I sensed that a few were sneering at his powerless grief. I sensed cynics wondering why he hadn't come at once - if Lazarus meant so much to him. But I sensed something else. I sensed love and compassion. I saw Mary look up at him, and her tears finally ceased. As did mine. My thoughts were like a revelation. 'He's with us, in our grief. He's going there, to that desolate place of death, and he's taking the heaviest portion of it on himself.'

But if he felt my grief, he also felt my anger. His own voice was angry, as if he was angry not at the circumstances, but at death itself. "Roll the stone aside!" he ordered.

I was horrified. I couldn't stop myself from protesting. "Lord, he's been dead for four days. The smell will be terrible."

His piercing gaze swung round to me. "Didn't I tell you that you would see God's glory if you believe?"

I took a step back, silenced. His rebuke was fair. Hadn't I told him of my trust in him not half an hour earlier? My uncle looked at me questioningly as he stood by the stone to the cave, along with the others who had carried the bier. Bewildered, but knowing that Jesus would not order such a thing for no reason, I nodded. They rolled the stone away. It was heavy. It took three of them, straining hard, to move it.

Jesus prayed loudly a prayer of thanksgiving which I barely heard – my eyes were on the dark hole of the open tomb. And then he shouted an order, in a voice full of power and authority.

"Lazarus, come out!"
'What?' I thought. 'How could he? He was dead!' Yet a wild hope

had been birthed. I knew it was impossible, of course, but I shaded my eyes all the same and stared at the darkness within the cave. Out he came! After four days! Called back from heaven alone knows where! My mind refused to accept the evidence of my eyes. He walked slowly, with the linen strips unravelling as he came. My first ridiculous, protesting thought was, 'We bound him tightly – we bound his legs together, he shouldn't be able to move.' Let alone the fact that Lazarus was actually alive under the burial cloths! Others were not so sure. As he emerged, there was a collective gasp of shock that I could physically feel. There was fear. There was a stunned silence. Jesus, who had wept, and then shouted, now had laughter in his voice as he instructed, in what had to be his most unnecessary instruction ever, "Unwrap him and let him go."

Mary was the first to move. She sprung up and stumbled towards the figure. Her hands pulled at his neck and freed the head cloth, whipping it off with a cry of joy. It was Lazarus. My beloved brother, with tousled hair and his big brown eyes, looking bemused and a little scared. His eyes searched the crowd. I thought he was looking for me, and I was about to call out when I saw his gaze settle on Jesus. Lazarus's face was serious now – he looked awestruck. Jesus' smile was wide and warm as he sat down on the rough grass and watched as we hastened to rip the clothes of death from our brother.

I had been quite wrong. There was no horrible smell. No smell at all. As I pulled off my veil I noticed that my hands, which had been stained from soaking the linen in the ointment those four days ago, were clean. The smell had instantly left them too. When we returned to the house, singing as we went, the smell had gone from there as well. The smell of death was banished from our lives entirely. The man who was the Resurrection and the Life had taken it away, for he was our friend.

He cared deeply about us and every aspect of our lives, and always had done. I never doubted it again.

■■'

Meditation

Imagine the shock, the wonder, the gratitude of Lazarus' family after he rose from the dead. Our familiarity with the story can blind us to the awesome nature of such an event.

Even though Jesus alone knew the positive outcome to follow, he wept when he saw the grief of the mourners. Even when he has the answers, he does not always rush to fix things. He first identifies with our pain.

Poem - Freedom Fighter

A knight in shining armour
rescues his damsel but once
and it is finished.

But You
You delight in spectacular rescues time and again
from history's dawn
to countless tomorrows,
as the odds stack up against Your loved ones
In You come
again and again
sweeping Your enemies aside like dust
You swoop to their rescue -
Moses - helpless and newborn, about to be murdered
Joseph - forgotten and rotting in prison
Gideon - outnumbered and trembling in the wine-press
David - nomadic and exiled - You made him king
You saved them -
Peter from jail
Adam from himself
Lazarus from the grave
Paul from shipwreck
Me from
darkness.

You break the chains off
Never failing to respond to Your children's cries for help

Except once.

Only once did You turn away
when the wall of sin willingly borne
prevented Your intervention.

150

As Your child looked up
And cried for help
"My God, My God, why have You forsaken me?"
You did not reply.
What price that silence?
What pain tore through Your heart
even as His was torn with spear?
There You were
The ultimate freedom fighter
Your hands tied
by Yourself.
Your hands pierced
by us.
Yet even then
As death stole You away,
freedom groaned
and stirred
even from the life-giver's grave.

It took three days
before You burst through
wild and free.
A hole rent through death's doorway
never to be repaired.
A path forged
to eternity
for all who will follow

Ultimate triumph
death defeated.

Freedom won
forever
for all who would receive it.

It is finished!
151

Martha's Story Part 3: Mary

Lazarus was alive! Though I saw him and held him, I could hardly believe the evidence before me. Eventually we left the burial place. It was the happiest journey of my life. That walk – and it was not far – from the tombstones back to our home. That happy hour!

What a mixture of joy, awe, wonder and shock we felt as we unwrapped the bindings from Lazarus. As soon as his hands were free, he helped, until he stood there, in the simple linen tunic that Dara had found some four days earlier. I clutched his arm and would not – could not – let it go. My brother was back! I laughed, I cried, I wanted to run the length and breadth of Judah with him, crying to the world, 'Look! My brother is alive! Four dark days he was dead, and now he lives! See what Jesus has done!'

As it was, I simply held on to his arm, speechless. We stared in disbelief at the healthy pink skin underneath. Not only was he alive, but he looked so well – as if he had never been ill. If anything, he looked more alive than he had ever done. He was vibrant. There were long embraces between the three of us, but of course others were there too. People had hung back when we were unwinding his bindings, but once they were discarded, all his relatives and friends drew closer, wanting to see, not quite daring to touch, and not sure what to say to a man who had been dead for four days.

It was my young cousin, Sara, who eventually broke the awkwardness by blurting out the question in everyone's minds, "What was it like? Being... gone? And coming back again? What was it like?"

I had not been able to see Jesus through the crowds, but now he moved closer. I saw him, and I saw Lazarus look at him. A long, wordless look of understanding seemed to pass between them. Lazarus reached out a hand and cupped Sara's cheek.

"It was like nothing I can express." His eyes returned to Jesus. "One day I will go back." For a second there was regret in his voice, as if he had been wrenched away from something intensely precious and wonderful. But then his eyes returned to us, and he looked with joy upon those he loved. He drew Mary and me to himself – one on either side - hugging each of us. "Ah, but I'm hungry!" he exclaimed, and I laughed in delight, finding words at last.

"Then we shall feast now! Our fast shall be transformed into a feast! Come!"

At last we moved, arms still around one another. What a procession we made! Usually those who returned from the graves moved slowly, reluctant to leave loved ones behind. They were downcast, mournful and weeping. Not us! Not that day! Was there ever such a noisy, joyful group to return from that grim place? We came with laughter and loud voices. Not everyone from Bethany had been there, and those who had remained at home emerged as we passed to see what all the noise was about. I can still picture them – shock, fear, disbelief, amazement and wonder on every face.

There was an unspoken, open invitation for everyone to return with us, though some took the road to Jerusalem, eager to spread the word within the city about this mighty miracle that Jesus had wrought. What power he wielded! I believe that at that moment he could have persuaded the people to do anything. He could have marched into the temple and deposed Caiaphas, the high priest. He could have deposed anyone. He could have claimed Herod's throne – maybe even challenged Pontius Pilate himself – for who else could wield power over life and death? Even the Romans - in all their might - seemed a puny force beside Jesus, who could tame winds, restore sight to the blind, and break the power of death itself. We had heard rumours that he had done this before, but only shortly after someone – a child, I believe – had died. Some said she was not truly dead. But to see it for ourselves! And Lazarus had been in the grave for four whole days. There was no doubt. Even if you didn't like what he was doing, you couldn't deny his power. But how could anyone not like it? For his miracles were born of compassion and executed with love. Who could turn away from such love?

Jesus returned with us, but he hung back, walking quietly beside a couple of his friends. He seemed subdued. At the time, I assumed that performing such a miracle had drained him of power and that he was simply tired. People left him alone - I think many were awed and even a bit fearful of him. The focus was on Lazarus. He led the way back, periodically throwing an arm around me or Mary – we walked on either side of him. We sang some of David's psalms of praise as we went. It was a noisy crowd who returned to the house at Bethany. I raced ahead, calling for Dara.

"Dara, bring out all the food you can find! The fast is over now!"

Dara and Abdown came out of the house at our call, and stared beyond us in shock.

"Of course – you've not seen!"

Lazarus laughed at their faces and approached, still clad only in the linen burial shift.

"I'm not a ghost! See what Jesus has done. He called me back..." There was wonder in his voice, which tailed off as he looked around for Jesus. But Jesus was lost somewhere in the mass of people who thronged around.

The chaos had begun. We were not to have a moment to ourselves for many days.

We celebrated all day. A procession of people visited us, mainly from Bethany, having heard the news and wanting to see for themselves. Gradually, after the initial shock had passed, people started to approach Lazarus, to touch him, to speak with him - albeit a little awkwardly at first. My brother's natural shyness seemed to have fallen away like the linen strips we had pulled off him. He joked with people, putting them at their ease.

They came to see Jesus too, though few dared approach him. In my excitement I barely noticed how quiet he was that day. If I did, again, I put it down to tiredness. Surely such a miracle would exhaust a man. Yet he did not sleep, or even doze. He sat, leaning against a wall, an untouched goblet of wine by his side. He ate little, accepting only a flat slab of bread, which he broke, and broke again. It remained uneaten on his lap, as his hands played with it and it gradually disintegrated into crumbs. His eyes seemed both far away one minute and watchful the next. A smile played around his eyes when he watched Lazarus, myself or Mary, but then his gaze would grow distant, and he almost looked sad in unguarded moments. But I had no time to ponder these things, for I was caught up in the joy of this resurrection in front of us.

155

How carefully I used to plan feasts, but this night, everything we could find just came out and was eaten. I instructed Dara to head to the market first thing the next morning to get more supplies in.

It was late at night that people finally started to depart - was it only this same day that we had wept our way to the tombs? Those who had followed him from Jerusalem, returned there. Our relatives stayed, as did Jesus and the men.

It was hard to sleep. The exhilaration of the day still pumped through my veins as I relived that incredible moment when Lazarus had emerged from the tomb. Finally, exhaustion took over, and I think I fell asleep in the early hours of the morning, still smiling as I slept.

It seemed only a minute later that I stirred, disturbed by a noise. I sat up and looked across to Mary's bed. She was already awake, and sat at the window. I looked out, and saw a shadow move in the darkness.

"What is it?" I whispered. She did not look around but continued staring outside. It was not pitch black. The sun had not yet risen but the sky had become a little paler.

"Jesus," she whispered back. Of course. He would often rise early and walk. He prayed as he went, no doubt. Sometimes he would be gone for hours. It was often his only chance of any solitude. Mary looked round. In the pale gloom her eyes looked black and seemed huge.

Now, for the first time since Lazarus had risen, I felt a strange foreboding. The joy of knowing my brother lived was still there, but something disturbed me.

"What is it?" I repeated. I knew Mary felt it too. She sighed, and shook her head.

"I don't know", she whispered. "Jesus... is... something has changed."

It was only now that I really considered how he had been the previous night. He had been quiet. John, also quiet, had sat near him, most of the evening. Was something happening? I rose.

"We'll have more visitors today, as the word spreads. I'm going to make more bread." I rose and swiftly moved to the kitchen. As I worked, I laughed quietly at myself. I had naively assumed that once the fuss had died down our lives might return to normal, but it was just starting to dawn on me that any normality had been left at the tombs, along with the linen rags and Lazarus' shyness. Things had irrevocably changed. Eventually we would realise that this miracle, which had seemed to be a free and generous gift at the time, came at a huge cost. Yet it was Jesus who paid the highest price.

But even with Dara, Abdown, our cousins and ourselves working hard to get in food and bake endless supplies of bread, it was impossible to be as hospitable as I would have liked to all who visited us over the next few days. It seemed that every person in Bethany called upon us, and soon they were followed by people from Jerusalem as well.

They came to see Lazarus – had he truly been dead so long? How could such a miracle be possible? The questions would inevitably lead to Jesus, and people would become quiet as they regarded such an ordinary looking man with such extra ordinary power. This man, who I believed was our Messiah, who could silence a thunderstorm, made all the questions on a hundred lips die away into awed silence.

The consequences of this resurrection did not die away. Our relatives returned to their home in Jerusalem, only for our Uncle Jethro to return the following evening. He looked worried. Late in the evening, when the stream of visitors had stopped flowing, he called us to one side.

"You need to be careful. You cannot imagine what an effect all this is having in Jerusalem."

I frowned. "What do you mean, Uncle? Jesus is widely known for his miracles." I was slow to understand. This was like no other miracle.

My uncle shook his head. "Martha — Jesus has not just healed a man with a limp here. His power has frightened some powerful men. Men whose power is not in miracles, but in politics and manipulation. This miracle," he put an arm around Lazarus. "This wonderful miracle." He paused to clear his throat. "This has happened too near to Jerusalem, where these men of 'power' have their seats. It has happened too close to the Passover, when the city is full of many who come to worship God. People come to pray for the end of their oppression and the tyranny of the Romans. They pray for the Messiah to come. The religious leaders are terrified that these people will start looking to Jesus. For if he can restore someone who was dead, what else might he be able to do? Who could stand against him? The religious leaders are dangerous when they are terrified. They are plotting."

I was starting to understand — so slowly my mind worked this day! Too overwhelmed by recent events.

Mary stood quietly. She seemed very calm as she spoke clearly, "It's not safe here."

I wasn't sure what she meant, even so. "For whom?"

"For Jesus – and for Lazarus," replied Jethro. He looked at his nephew affectionately, with concern in his eyes. "My son, I fear some of them are plotting to kill you."

"What!!" I was aghast. "Why? What Jesus has done is wonderful! How could anyone want to...?" Tears welled up and I could speak no more.

My uncle came to me now, and embraced me. He spoke as if talking to a child. "Martha – since when have all men been good? Jesus is good, and his goodness challenges powerful men. Now they see that this goodness wields such power – they are scared. They want to discredit him. Hide the evidence of his power – and if that means killing Lazarus, and hiding the body - alas I fear some might stoop so low. Of course we will not let that happen, but I had to warn you."

Jesus spoke up. I hadn't realised he'd been listening. He was sitting, a little way off, staring into the fire that was lit in the yard. I wondered fleetingly how he'd heard, for my uncle had been keeping his voice low.

"Tomorrow," said Jesus, "We're leaving. " There was something in his voice. An infinite sadness. It killed the protest that rose on my lips.

It was Peter who asked, "Where will we go next? To the city?" He seemed eager to go to Jerusalem, even as Thomas nearby was shaking his head. Jesus, though, also shook his head. "Not yet.

There is still time before the Passover. We will prepare. We'll go to Ephraim."

No one argued, though several of them looked mystified, and some disappointed. Mary crossed to him and sat beside him. They sat there for a while, but it was not long before Jesus stood. He rested a hand briefly on her head before making his way into the house where he would sleep.

Judas spoke up petulantly, brave enough to challenge him now that he was no longer there. "Ephraim," he grumbled, "What's in Ephraim?" What was it about Judas that made me uneasy? I knew I was not alone in my distrust of him. He seemed to rub several of the other disciples up the wrong way. Yet others of them argued amongst themselves as well. Jesus was no fool; he must have had his reasons for selecting these men to be his disciples. It was Peter who replied impatiently, "There's nothing in Ephraim. It's a wilderness."

"Perhaps that's the point," said John softly, with a quiet smile.

I sighed and turned back to my uncle. "What about Lazarus? Should he go too?"

Lazarus himself spoke up. "I'll stay. It's not really me that they are after."

So he stayed. Jesus and his men left at first light. Even so, afterwards, people again started arriving. My heart and mood had changed overnight. Yesterday I was delighted that so many had come. I wanted them to share our joy, to see for themselves what Jesus was capable of doing. I didn't care who they were or where they were from. Anyone was welcome. But now it was different.

A shadow had fallen. I was still pleased to see our neighbours from Bethany. Many of them had already visited, but they returned, wanting to check that Lazarus was still feeling well. But today I noticed just how many of our visitors were strangers. I tried to question them. Were they on their way to prepare for the feast at Jerusalem, or had they come from the city? People always came to Jerusalem weeks before the Passover. Those who travelled the furthest would only make the trek once a year, not attending the lesser feasts there, in order to make the most of their time. They would use the opportunity to visit friends and family. Once I had established who was from the city, these were the people I was wary of. I noted their reaction when they saw my brother. If it was joy or wonder, I relaxed. But some seemed fearful or thoughtful, or even cynical. These I watched like a hawk to assess whether or not they might be a threat. I grew particularly concerned if they also asked, 'And where is this Jesus?' I confess that my smile of welcome became strained as the day went on.

Lazarus seemed unconcerned, and was willing to talk to any who wanted. He had a new found confidence, and few could argue with his experience. Gradually, though, as the days passed, the visitors became fewer. I still dared to hope that our lives might return to normal. Yet the sense of danger that came with my uncle's visit did not disperse even as our visitors dwindled in number. It grew in my mind. It grew every time I heard Jesus discussed. 'Who was he?' was the unanswered question I heard on more and more lips. It was a question asked in equal measures of hope and fear. Was I the only one who felt an increasing sense of dread? I watched my siblings, puzzled. It was as if Mary and Lazarus had swopped personalities. Mary's girlish outbursts of

161

enthusiasm grew fewer by the day. Her easy laugh had been silenced. She grew quiet and thoughtful. Even when doing tasks around the house, she was preoccupied. Lazarus, on the other hand, had shed his shyness and reticence. Now he was the one who would laugh openly, albeit a quiet, contented laugh. The mischief, previously hidden much of the time, was now much in evidence. He teased each one of us. We smiled at his antics, but when his attention turned away the laughter died on our lips. We were waiting, and we did not know what for. The heat grew more oppressive than ever.

A few days later and it was just one week until the Passover. That was the day Andrew arrived. He took me to one side. "Make preparations, but make them quietly. Jesus wants to dine here tomorrow, but just with the family."

"He is going to the Passover then?" I asked with dread in my heart, knowing the answer. Andrew simply nodded, his expression unreadable. He knew, as we all did, that they were walking into danger.

I thought about what to serve. I remembered that first feast I had laid before Jesus. Such an abundance of food served with pride but with such a paucity of love. Tomorrow's food would be far simpler, but served with much more love.

It was good to have something to do, a task to occupy us. Mary worked quietly preparing the date and fig cakes. Dara and I baked bread and prepared dishes of lentils, beans and vegetables.

He arrived in the afternoon, when the streets were quiet. This was a time when we would not spill outside and make a merry commotion. The moment I saw his face I knew something had

162

changed. Jesus himself had this same feeling of foreboding as us. It might not be obvious to those who didn't know him well, but I could see it in small ways. In the way he grasped our hands in greeting, just a little harder and longer than usual. He didn't doze, as he often did on his visits. He stayed awake and said little, but watched everything. He watched his men talking noisily about the coming Passover. They, too, seemed to expect something to happen, but they appeared full of excitement rather than dread. He watched Lazarus who was right in the middle of them, full of life. He watched me. I was happy, as always, to work in the kitchen with the food. As I caught his eye, I was reminded again of his first visit when I fussed and bustled around like an angry bee. I worked just as hard now, but it was with calmness and peace. He smiled warmly at me suddenly, and I wondered if he also was thinking of that same day. I could almost read the words in his eyes, 'My dear Martha'. This time, Mary did not sit at his feet. She was not even in the room. I wondered suddenly where she had got to. I was about to go and look for her when I noticed the men were running out of wine, and by the time I had served more, I had forgotten about her absence.

She appeared after they had finished eating, after the dishes were tidied away, when the men sat relaxing on the floor mats. She looked amazing. She had changed into a clean robe. It was her best – a simple blue robe with clean cut lines. She had unbraided and uncovered her hair. I smiled inwardly when I saw it – knowing that that sight alone would horrify our relatives, and would have horrified me not that long ago! It was a wanton thing to do in our society. But there was nothing wanton about her. In her hands she clutched tightly her jar of perfume, holding the main part with one hand, and the lid with the other. She had already broken open the lid, I realised, and I could smell the rich scent as she passed me. She did not even look at me; her eyes were moist with tears and fixed on Jesus.

The men had all stopped talking, and a deep silence fell on the room as they stared at Mary. Without hesitating, she knelt on the floor by Jesus and started to pour out the perfume, massaging it into his feet.

I was mesmerised. I was witnessing an act of intimate love. Somehow, though, in spite of Mary's gentle touch, and every movement expressing deep love, there was nothing sexual about the act. It was pure love poured out. It was sacrificial, too – that perfume was expensive! We were well off by most people's standards, but even we would not be able to throw away a year's wages, which was what the perfume was worth. Not only that. It would have been part of Mary's wedding dowry, perhaps to be used on the very day she would be a bride. Maybe that added to the sense of intimacy, but seeing Mary anointing Jesus like this did not make me think of a wedding. It reminded me instead of the night, not long ago, when together we had anointed the body of our beloved brother for burial. When our love was overwhelmed by grief. I became aware of tears trickling down my face as I watched.

Mary tipped her head forward and began wiping the excess perfume away with her loose, silky hair. The fragrance had permeated into every corner of the room. The smell was heavy, and so strong that I almost felt dizzy. As I watched, it was as if I too were feeling the love which was being poured out as freely as the perfume. Jesus said not one word. He didn't move an inch. His head was bowed. He simply received what Mary was giving.

No one dared to break the spell with either words or movement. Yet out of the corner of my eye I became aware of something. Someone's head moved. I was being watched. I glanced left, moving only my eyes and saw that it was Judas. He was staring at me with what looked like anger. He was urging me with his eyes, as if he wanted me, as the eldest in the house, to do or say something. To stop Mary, perhaps.

But this wasn't even about Mary by now. I deliberately turned slightly away from Judas, and once again regarded my sweet sister pouring out her heart. All of us who loved Jesus, were we all feeling the same thing? I felt as if it were my hands, too, anointing his feet. My heart was crying out, 'I love you too. I would pour out all I have for you.'

Jesus' head remained bowed. Mary had just about finished, but she remained in quiet submission by his feet. The silence was deep, reverent and profound.

It was Judas who broke it in the ugliest of ways. His voice sounded harsh and angry. He objected - he actually objected - to what had been happening,

"That perfume was worth a year's wages! It should have been sold and the money given to the poor!"

Heads swivelled to stare at him. I was angry. This man had dined here before. He had received our hospitality on many occasions, and here he was, accusing my sister, whose heart was as exposed as if it were lying on a slab on the floor. Mary's whole body winced, as if she had received a physical blow. I looked around to see the other men weighing Judas' words. Most, like me, frowned, but one or two were looking thoughtful, maybe even starting to nod in agreement.

Before I, or anyone else, could open their mouth to object, in the space of a heartbeat, Jesus' head had snapped up. His eyes burned with anger as he challenged Judas. "Leave her alone. She did this in preparation for my burial. You will always have the poor among you, but you will not always have me."

His hand had moved to rest gently but firmly on Mary's shoulder as he spoke, in a gesture of reassurance. His anger was not aimed at her. He carried on in defence of Mary, who simply looked down at the floor. It made me think of a mother lion defending her young.

"She has done what she could. I tell you the truth, wherever the Good News is preached throughout the world, this woman's deed will be remembered and discussed."

There was pride and appreciation in his voice now. He spoke as if she had done something to change the world, yet all she had done was to pour out her heart in a simple act of pure love.

Judas had no reply to that. He turned away, still angry.

I wondered what Jesus meant. A frisson of excitement ran through me when he spoke of Good News spreading throughout the world. Was this perhaps the time when he was going to declare himself Messiah? Were the days of obscurity, of wandering through the remote regions of Israel, drawing to a close? He had certainly never been so sought out in Bethany before, though Lazarus' resurrection had a lot to do with that. He'd only been here a few hours and I noticed that others were gathering now. Our house was filling up again. The intimate moment had passed. There would be little privacy now.

He remained the next day. People came once more and the house could barely contain them. We were rapidly running out of food again, but I knew that he wouldn't stay long. Uncle Jethro again came from the city. He said that he had never known a Passover like it. There was expectation and excitement in the air, and the word on everyone's lips was, 'Jesus'. The priests were furious about his popularity. They saw him as a direct threat. My uncle had managed to get Jesus alone at one point, so he told me.

"I told him − 'it's dangerous for you there.' I urged him to be careful."

"What did he say?"

Jethro sighed. "Nothing. He simply looked at me with compassion, as if I was the one in danger and needing reassurance. He just drew me back into the room where everyone else was. I couldn't pursue it there - I don't know who all these people are and I'm reluctant to talk openly in front of them."

"He knows, Uncle. I've watched him. He knows that something is about to happen, to change. Sometimes I think he fears it a little, but whatever happens, it won't be a surprise to him. I've felt it coming, this change. It's as if clouds were gathering before a storm. I feel it here." I struck my breast bone, and heard the tremble in my voice. There was nothing my uncle could say. He embraced me, holding me close for a long time. It reminded me of the comfort he had brought when my father had died.

My aunt appeared.

"Martha, my dear," she smiled, seeing me there with her husband. "I have to ask you. What have you used in the house? I've never smelt such a sweet fragrance. I can barely smell the sweat of the men, even in the crowded rooms - which is saying something in this heat! I've looked for hidden posies of flowers or leaves, which I know Mary loves to use, but I can see nothing. But that fragrance, it permeates everything. What is it?"

I smiled, blinking back the moistness in my eyes. I was about to tell her about the anointing, but hesitated. Words could not express that moment, and I wanted no misunderstanding of it. Besides, I thought, that was yesterday. With all the visitors we had had, that fragrance should have dispersed by now. My aunt was right – it was still strong.

I shook my head in the end and replied helplessly, "I think it's no earthly fragrance. It's the smell of love and worship." I breathed deeply and smelt it anew.

It was early the following day when Jesus took his leave. The visitors had mostly gone to their homes the night before, and he was leaving before any more arrived this day. He embraced me that morning and, once again, the rich scent enveloped me. He put a hand on my head and murmured a blessing. Finally he stood back and looked at me with such love that I was undone. Tears spilled over, and he put a hand on my cheek to brush them away. He smiled so kindly. "My dear Martha," he said softly, as if he knew how much those three words meant to me, and it was all I could do not to sob. Somehow I felt finality in his farewell, though I tried to tell myself I was being ridiculous. Surely he would come back and visit again?

Mary could not let him go. She declared her intention to go with them to Jerusalem, and I didn't have the heart to stop her. There would be other women there to take care of her. I stood in the doorway, watching the small band go towards Jerusalem. People were already emerging to watch them pass.

There were many questions I had planned on asking him, but in the end I asked none of them. I sit here, slowing writing down my memories. I wonder what lies ahead. The house is quiet. Lazarus rests in his room. The servants are clearing up the debris of yesterday, and I am alone with my thoughts.

The house still smells of the sweet fragrance. I wonder if it will always be with us. Mary, a simple girl, poured out her precious love, and the fragrance was spilled out. Somehow it has mingled with the love for Jesus that poured out of, and still pours out of, my heart. Perhaps it will pour out of many other hearts and become a fragrance that is released across the entire world until the end of time itself.

I wish I had asked him that one question that burns in my heart.

"Do you go to face your doom or your destiny?"

But I suspect that if I had, he would have just looked at his dear Martha with that enigmatic smile of his, and replied, "Yes."

■■■

Meditation

Mary's worship was love poured out with extravagant abundance. So often mine is stilted or held back and restrained. Dare to let your heart be poured out before him. Maybe put on some music that draws you to Him and join in the song. Let your heart go. Let the love flow.

Poem - Worship

At your feet Lord Jesus
I can think of no better place
to be

breaking open my heart
releasing the love inside
pouring it over your feet
I can think of no better thing to do

to touch your feet
soon to be pierced with my sin
to dry them with my hair
bowing down
I can think of no greater joy

letting all I am
pour forth
all over you.

Spectators beware
it's a shocking sight - this wholehearted givenness
embarrassing - this emotion
messy - this pouring out
can such excess be religious?

But even as you object to the master
he will rise and protect me
his look cuts to your heart - revealing all - silencing you
with barely a word.

Jesus
your feet remain safe in my hands
my heart remains safe in yours.

Lazarus's story: Bethany

I woke up in the night. I often did these days.

Sometimes I would stay there, but more often I would rise and go
to the courtyard. The palms and foliage there released their scent
at night- it was a fragrant place. I would sit there, or meander
around slowly, thinking and remembering.

That night I rose quietly and went to the courtyard, expecting to
find it as empty as usual. "It must be well past midnight," I
thought.

I was surprised to see the fire was still burning. Occasionally the
embers might still have retained some heat or even been glowing,
but more often it would have died down completely by now.

Then I saw him. Yeshua. Lit up by the flickering flames, lying on
the ground on his side, his elbow bent, his head resting on his
hand, gazing at the fire. He was very still. I hesitated, wondering
whether to tiptoe away and leave him on his own. They had been
to Jerusalem today, and there seemed to be more on his mind
than usual. He had been quiet at supper.

But before I had a chance to move, his head turned and he saw
me. He beckoned me over with his free hand. Still hesitant I
walked around the fire, stood still and looked down at him.

"I don't want to disturb you. I woke... I... "

He brushed away my words with the hand that had beckoned me,
and in the flicker of the firelight I caught his smile. He said, softly,
"Lazarus. Sit."

I sunk to the floor and lay, like him, on my side. Our heads were close so that we could speak softly, without disturbing anyone. But I didn't know what to say. There was an intense feeling about him. In the end, I simply watched the fire. It smelt fragrant – aromatic – and I wondered abstractly which wood was being burned.

For a long time we sat in silence. Comfortable silence. Ever since it had happened – since he had called me back from the grave – I'd felt very close to this man. I had no brother, but he felt closer than a brother could have done. We'd never spoken together about it, but I knew he understood something of the place I had been to.

I'd not spoken with anyone about it. A few people had sometimes taken me aside and asked me, with morbid curiosity, what it was like to be 'on the other side'. Some, especially Martha, had begged me to describe heaven to her. But I couldn't. How could you describe such a place, such an experience? It would be like trying to describe beauty to someone blind from birth. The beauty of mountains, of a butterfly's wings, the colours of a rainbow, all to someone with no context to imagine such things. It was impossible. So I simply smiled, and shrugged, and shook my head. But looking at Yeshua, looking into his eyes at that moment by the grave.... he knew. I was certain he knew, and it created a deep, unspoken bond between us. I felt closer to him than I had ever felt to a man.

I gazed into the flames, remembering the musical harmonies. The colours! The joy!

Eventually he spoke. For a second I was startled, for I had become lost in the silence. There was pain in his voice.
"We went to the temple today."

"Umm," I murmured. He had to know that I knew this – Peter and John had been talking about it over supper, and he'd been there.

He shifted, sitting cross legged now, so I sat up too, leaning back against the trunk of a palm.

He shook his head, and his voice almost sounded bewildered. "That they could do such things..."

His voice trailed off into silence again, but I was puzzled. What did he mean? The others had said nothing about anything unusual happening at the temple. What had been going on? I had been concerned when he had insisted on sticking to his plans to visit the city. Ever since he had called me back, rumours had been circling that the authorities were after him. They were frightened of a man who wielded such power. They wanted him stopped. What had happened?

"Yeshua?" I prompted. "What things?"

"I've been speaking with the Father about it. It's evil. Some come many miles on foot to seek their God, knowing of no other place where He can be found. And what do they find? Pandemonium. Cheats. Instead of love, they are met with greed. And some of those that come to seek – the Gentiles – aren't allowed to go in further, and that's all they see. Those things!" His voice had risen.

I tried to reassure him. "But Yeshua, most who come are believers. They know how it is. They can go further into the courts."

His head swivelled round to stare at me, and now there was a quiet anger in his voice. "And what of those who carefully pick the best of their flocks to sacrifice? Only to be told by the priests that there is some blemish on it and it is unacceptable."

174

"But isn't that why there are animals in the courts to be bought? They even sell the court currency there." I was puzzled. Why was Jesus so upset? It had always been so, at the temple. People knew the routine. You were foolish to bring your own animals, for more often than not the priests would find some imaginary fault with them. No. You brought your money, had it changed to the temple currency, and then bought the available animals for the sacrifices. He knew it was so.

"Lazarus!" His eyes seemed to burn at me. "Their exchange rates are extortionate. They cheat people. People who have no choice but to pay if they want their sins atoned. The animals are overpriced and often in a worse condition than those that they had brought from home. And the money changers and stall keepers shout over one another, trying to haggle for the best price. The most money! Why should the temple have its own currency, anyway? They have made it so purely to cheat people – and usually the poorest of people at that!" His voice grew sterner. "I have spoken with my Father. We will not have it. Our house should be a place of worship. Of prayer. But they have made it a..." he paused, and said the words severely and carefully, as if he were quoting someone else, "...den of thieves."

I knew he cared especially for the poor. I'd grown so used to the temple system that I barely noticed it when I went there these days. I would have thought he had got used to it too, though being on the road so much, he only came to Jerusalem for the big feasts. So perhaps it had struck him anew. It was always worse – noisier, and with higher prices – at the Passover.

I sighed. "Master," I pleaded, wanting his anger to subside. I knew he wasn't angry with me, but still I hated to see it. It was a little frightening, to be truthful. "You're right, of course. They do cheat people, and the poorest of people at that. I've become so used to it that it no longer strikes me. I have settled for it, I suppose. For what can be done?"

The fire that had blazed up in his eyes died down, but his voice remained deadly serious. "Something has to be done. We will not settle for the desecration of our House. It's the only place where people know they can come in worship, to find God himself, at the moment... it must be restored."

"But how?" I asked. I hated his distress. I had reached back and twisted off a frond of the palm I had been leaning against while we had been speaking. I had been fiddling with it, ripping it into strips, and then weaving the strips together. He reached over and took the plaited leaves from me. I had woven them tightly and they resembled a whip. He held one end and swished it through the air.

"They must go," he said quietly, and swished the whip again. "I must drive them out."

I was horrified. I stared at him. My hand shot out and grasped his arm tightly. "You can't do such a thing! You'll be arrested! They're just waiting for the smallest excuse as it is. This would push them over the edge..." Tears started to well up unbidden in my throat. I loved this man. I couldn't bear the thought of harm coming to him. I knew from his disciples about the dark words he kept speaking about being betrayed, arrested, and even killed. I couldn't bear it.

He put his free hand on top of my white knuckles, where I was clutching him.

"Peace, Lazarus." His touch was still warm, though by now the fire had died down. Now I could feel the slight chill in the night air.

Beside me, Yeshua had tipped back his head and was staring into the skies. I found myself doing the same. He moved his hand from over mine and pointed upwards, speaking softly.

"Look! See the stars. Can you see the Bear?" His fingers drew the constellation in the dark air. One by one he started naming the constellations, and then the stars which formed them. I loved it when he spoke like this. It was as if I were a child and he were reading me a bedtime story to quiet me.

How did he know all their names? And how could he tell them all apart? He knew so much about everything. He always had. His mother told me that even as a child he had known far more than other children. He seemed to soak up knowledge from everything around him.

My neck was aching so I let go of his arm and lay back on the ground, edging closer to the glowing embers. I gazed up at the skies. Still he carried on, naming star after star.

His words washed over me and at some point I drifted towards sleep. I was aware of his voice, but could no longer make out what he was saying. Was he speaking to me, or to himself, or was he perhaps praying? At some point I remember thinking that he must have been speaking in a different language, but then I heard the words, "See the lights shining in the darkness? The darkness will never overcome them."

Then came the music. I'm not sure if I was hearing it anew, or whether I was simply remembering the music of heaven. But it was back with me. It filled my soul, mingling with the sound of his voice, and it felt for all the world that he was singing over me with love.

It's a sound that has never left me. It is strongest at night or in my darkest hours, and always it reminds me that love is stronger than death. That his love is stronger than anything.

Meditation

That story is totally from my imagination. Of course, what is said about the temple is true, but we are told nothing about such an encounter between Jesus and Lazarus.

What must it have been like, those last days with Jesus? His friends must have been aware of the danger Jesus was in.

For now they did the best thing possible – they stuck close to him, listening to all he said, though they didn't understand much of what he said. Are you ever fearful? Do you face trials ahead? Take comfort in the knowledge that Jesus has faced everything ahead of you. The same source of courage and strength that he found is available to you, for the same holy Spirit dwells in you. Think about that as you pray for courage. His Spirit is within you.

Poem - Fear

Sometimes a raging screaming monster
Sometimes a quiet steel trap deep in my heart
Fear lives in darkness
and feeds on pain.

Fear denies the power of His love
And loves to deny His power

Fear is a gag around my mouth
paralyses my legs
my lips sealed shut
An ever tightening band, restricting my heart.

Fear lies
and calls us to trust it.
Fear promises to keep me safe
yet every time I yield to those velvet lies
I am seduced more into captivity

Fear warns me, in menacing words
of the dangers of RISK.
of the futility of dreams.
It promises to cover me and others
with a blanket of protection
failing to mention that the blanket
will suffocate us all in the end.

Oh, I hate fear
Though sometimes you would think I love it
so reluctant am I to let it go
So I sit, cold yet secure, within the dark walls of its cave.

But who is this approaching?
Light shining from His very being.....

Looking in and seeing me...
Love in His eyes, arms outstretched.
Pierced hands beckoning me come...

He does not enter, simply waits
Fear is a place He does not dwell in.
He conquered it once, and that was enough.
He beckons me come, tells me to trust

and it is up to me now...

Oh help me, Lord, for I am afraid.

Andrew's story: The Last Supper

It was a peaceful evening.

It was growing dark outside.

We were gathered – his twelve closest - with Jesus in the upper
room. It was Passover. It was not an entirely new situation. After
all, this was the third year in a row that we had travelled to
Jerusalem to celebrate the Passover feast. It was part of our
routine – this annual pilgrimage to celebrate the salvation of God.

Yet something felt different this year.

Even before we had entered the city, Jesus had been talking
about his death. His words grew strange - he was talking about
returning to the Father. He spoke of betrayal. He even rebuked
Peter - crying 'Get behind me, Satan' - when Peter tried to protest
about his morbid predictions.

Then there was the strange anointing at Bethany a week before
the Passover. It had reminded us of the time when the woman -
the prostitute - had appeared at Simon the Pharisee's house and
washed Jesus' feet. But this was more intense. For a start it was
Mary, someone very dear to Jesus, who had performed the
anointing. And the perfume she used was costly.

We had watched, astonished, as she broke open the alabaster jar
and poured the contents over Jesus' feet. It was as if she had
broken open her heart and was pouring out her love. It was an
intimate act, and we felt uncomfortable. What was she doing?
The air grew heavy with the intense scent.

It was Judas who broke the silence with a petty complaint about waste. Then a disagreement arose between Jesus and Judas, culminating in Jesus saying that it was an anointing prior to his burial.

What was this talk about death? We grew ever more uneasy.

And then there was Jerusalem - and the crowds! Each year, as Jesus' fame had spread, the crowds had grown more demanding, more desperate for wisdom, signs and healings. But this year they were overwhelming. This year when he arrived, they had waited for him on the road. They had ripped off branches from nearby trees and thrown them down on the road in front of him. Those who didn't have branches threw down their cloaks. A strange carpet of welcome for a carpenter on a donkey. The crowd had shouted their praises and the city was in uproar.

In previous years, Jesus had implied beforehand that he wasn't going to Jerusalem, but had then crept quietly in unnoticed. He didn't appear in public until he arrived to teach at the temple. Or, if he healed someone, he had urged people to 'say nothing' (as if you could keep quiet about such things!)

But no. This year he marched straight into the temple and started overturning tables, creating a rumpus about the dishonest trading that went on in God's house. Not only the traders, but the Pharisees, priests and elders were all furious with him. Furious at the disruption. Furious at the adulation he was receiving, and scared of the power and authority he wielded. A cauldron of trouble was brewing – we could all feel it coming to the boil, and we were powerless to stop it.

So, in this tense atmosphere, we sat at the Passover feast. We ate the sacrificial lamb even as Jesus spoke about the bread being like his sacrificial body. We drank the cups of wine even as Jesus spoke of the wine being like his shed blood. Our wine-addled brains were confused. Somewhere outside, we knew, there were volatile mobs who wanted so much from Jesus. Somewhere outside there were furious and powerful religious leaders who were ready to kill him if they got the chance. And, inside in this very room, there was unease amongst his friends as Jesus spoke again about some of us denying and betraying him.

Underneath it all were these constant references to his impending death. Every time he said something about it, it troubled our minds. It seemed to be in the very air around us like an oppressive fog.

And through it all, through all the arguments, fear and unease, John leant back, resting his head on the chest of Jesus. Even as, yet again, Jesus referred to one of us – his twelve closest friends – betraying him – John was relaxed. He knew his love went too deep to betray Jesus.

On Jesus' words about betrayal, the rest of us sat up straighter, looking around at each other in suspicion. Who could Jesus mean? Judas perhaps, although Thomas and one or two others – even Peter - looked uneasy. I myself was racking my brain to figure out if Jesus had any reason to accuse me.

But John leant back into the very body of Christ. Trusting. At rest. He didn't look as if he understood any more than the rest of us. But he trusted. He rested.

It was a peaceful evening.

It was dark outside.

Unbeknownst to us, Gethsemane and Golgotha were waiting.

Meditation

Spend time, like John, resting in the presence of Jesus. Sometimes words are not needed. Simply being near him is enough.

Poem – Sit with me

Sit with me.
Sit in my presence.
Let my light dazzle and beautify
All that is around you.
Submit the pain
Submit the dark clouds to me.

And see how my touch transforms
And makes all things beautiful.
See how I am everywhere
See how I enfold you.
The world says you are alone
Yet I am all around
Surrounding you,
By your side
And always shining my light in you.

Jesus at prayer

There was a conversation between them. Jesus was still on the earth at the time – a man. Fully human. He had drawn away from the crowds, as he did regularly whenever he felt the need. He needed time with the Father. He needed to prepare himself for all that lay ahead, for his time on earth was growing short. He was in one of those solitary places – perhaps by a lake, or in a forest, or walking in one of the many hills.

He sensed the presence of the Father all around him – in the scent of the olive trees, in the breath of the wind, in the warmth of the sun. He could feel creation responding to the Creator – in the call of the birds overhead, in the rustling of the leaves – he could almost sense the olives ripening around him. He glanced at them. Soon they would be gathered. Soon they would be crushed. Like him.

The Spirit whispered in his heart, revealing details of what lay ahead. The love and the pain of the Father touched his heart deeply. Jesus felt as if he was seated in the Father's heart. The Spirit was in him and by him, speaking the Father's words, comforting him as he considered what was ahead. The three were one. Time passed slowly as fewer words were needed, and the three gazed at one other in mutual love and honour. Eventually Jesus stirred, and spoke to the Father,

"And then there is Simon Peter."

He had been praying for his friend, of course, ever since the Spirit had revealed exactly how Satan intended to 'sift him like wheat'. Jesus had prayed that Simon's faith would not fail. He prayed with tears, for he knew that many bitter tears lay ahead for Simon. Would his disciple choose the path of self-disgust and bury himself back in his fishing nets? Or would he remember all that Jesus had said, the many attempts to forewarn him and the others of his death? Would he mull over those things and allow hope to grow? Whichever way Simon Peter chose, it was going to be a bleak few days for him. For them all. Most of all for Jesus and his Father and the Spirit, of course, but for now, selfless as ever, they considered Simon Peter and the best way to restore his soul.

Jesus smiled suddenly, remembering. He spoke to the Father,

"He's not lacking in courage. I love that about him. Do you remember, he was the only one who thought of joining me on the water. The others were at first terrified and then exhilarated, but only Simon Peter thought of joining me."

The Father and Spirit smiled, also remembering, but then they grew quiet again. The Spirit whispered the Father's words. "And yet, in the dark, when you need him most, his courage will fail him. Three times. "

Samuel had heard God's call three times before responding correctly. Jesus himself had overcome the temptations of the enemy three times. Three years they had been together now. And the rooster would crow after Peter had denied all knowledge of Jesus. Three times.

"He will need to be restored," said Jesus. "Three times. How shall we do it, do you think?" There was no question of unforgiveness, of course, for the very love of the Father pulsed through Jesus' veins. Simon was forgiven before he had even done it. He was loved. All of the disciples were loved.

"I have shown them our love. Urged them to share it."

"They will draw together when it's over," confirmed the Father. "They will be frightened. They'll draw together for comfort. They'll be asking me to help them."

"As they'll be together when the ultimate help comes," said the Spirit, looking ahead.

"It's a good time for me to rejoin them – when they are together," said Jesus. "But Simon – he will need more than that. More than even seeing me. The three denials will have cut his heart deeply. Knowing that I live will thrill him, but the guilt will still lie there, like three walls, between us."

"Then there must be words," agreed the Spirit. "Words three times, spoken like hammers, to knock down the walls." He paused in excited communion with the Father, and then added, "Not just words of forgiveness, but words spoken three times by himself to confess his love for you, even as he will have denied you three times."

"Yes." Jesus grew eager now, anticipating the scene. "And I will speak - not just words affirming him, but words to set him on the road ahead. Words to commission. Three times." His heart was full of love. He knew the Father's agreement.

"Where would be the best place, do you think?" asked Jesus. He thought back over the last three years. With affection, he remembered seeing the big, obstinate fisherman for the first time on the shores of the Sea of Galilee. A captive audience, as Jesus had borrowed his boat to preach from. Simon Peter's reluctant agreement to cast his nets again, even after he had been fishing

188

all night. And his amazement at the huge haul of fish that followed – which birthed faith that had him on his knees declaring his unworthiness within minutes. Jesus remembered Simon Peter wanting to walk on the water. He remembered seeing the panic in the man's eyes as he had started to sink. Immediately Jesus had reached out – he could still feel the calloused hands holding on to his own for dear life. He thought of the loaves and the fishes that Peter had helped to distribute to the five thousand. He recalled the many journeys as they travelled the area, even going to Jerusalem for the feasts. Simon Peter had changed. There had been a time when the fisherman lived by the sea - never happier than when he could see it or smell it on the wind. It had been his first love – the sea. Now he was never happier than when Jesus was within sight. Now Jesus was his first love, and the denial would hit him hard. Jesus closed his eyes and spoke to the Father. "Let his faith endure." The Spirit nodded. Jesus knew his prayer would be answered.

"So, the restoration. I should speak with him alone. But not straight away when I first return. He needs to get over the shock first," Jesus said wryly.

"We will commission him." The Spirit spoke the Father's words. "He will be a changed man. We will rename him 'the rock', for he will be solid. He will never let you down again. He will be Peter."

"And we will do it three times," agreed Jesus. They all nodded. The three of them loved Peter. "We will do it..." And all three spoke the final words of agreement together... "over breakfast, with fish, by the sea."

Meditation

Do you ever let Jesus down? He sees failure as an opportunity for redemption. See how lovingly and carefully he planned the reconciliation with Peter. Don't hang back if you feel you've failed him. Come with humility and see how willingly he forgives, how he loves to restore.

Poem - Gethsemane

Jesus
How did You feel?
You told them You were going
You told them they would grieve.
Were you hinting when You said
"a time is coming when I will not pray for you,
you can pray yourselves"?

You reminded them of their love for You.
You told them that You were going.
You said they would be scattered
But that You, Jesus
would be
all alone
(Yet not alone, for your Father was with You).

WHY didn't they pray for You, Jesus?
For Heaven's sake

When you most needed them, they slept
while your anguished soul cried out.

Your sad question:
"Couldn't you watch with me even one hour?"

Grief is a lonely place.
You alone are there.

The three people sat quietly for a time, as if they were digesting a rich meal. Lydia and Miriam watched the man. His eyes had grown distant as he looked back at a life lived in another world.

Eventually he whispered, and his words echoed theirs.

"I met him in a field, on a hill."

There was a long silence, for there the similarity of their stories ended.

At some point his voice broke the silence again. He cleared his throat and continued.

"I had heard of him, of course. It was impossible for anyone living in Jerusalem not to have heard of him, over the three years of his ministry. He would come for one of the feasts or something. He would cause trouble. He would argue with the Pharisees. Cause a stir in the temple. He would claim to be from God and then break God's laws. But he would break them in a way that didn't seem wrong – like healing someone on the Sabbath. If the Pharisees objected, he would tie them in knots with clever arguments. And when everyone was all astir, wondering if he would challenge the Romans themselves, he would up and go. He would disappear into the wilderness, or back up north, and things would settle down again. Until the next time. But his stories remained behind, remembered and repeated by many. In my circle we would laugh at them. Especially at the one about the foolish man who was helped by the Samaritan. We used to say that the traveller got all he was asking for. He was foolish to travel alone on the dangerous roads to Jericho - everyone knew that bandits were in the hills there. When it got to the part of the story where he was robbed, we would laugh! We declared that that we were those robbers, and we were proud of it.

I knew that Jesus seemed to have a soft spot for the poor, and that upset me, though I wouldn't have admitted it. It made me strangely jealous. I used to wonder if things might have been different for me if a man like Jesus been around when I was growing up. But then I would shake off such fruitless thoughts. I was what my poverty had made me. Had I not turned to theft I would have starved by now – that was the truth of it. The road from petty theft to robbery with violence had not been so very long. There were always those among us who had gone a step further. It made me feel that what I did was not so very bad. I might steal from a man's house and think it was not so bad, as I did not hurt anyone, unlike the man standing next to me. And then, when I did go a step further, and robbed a traveller with violence, I would think it wasn't so bad, because I hadn't murdered anyone, unlike the man standing next to me. After a while I stopped thinking about my actions altogether. My conscience was deadened. I did what I had to do, in order to get what I wanted. Others simply had more than me, and that wasn't fair. So I took what they had. I lived for the moment. A band of us tended to work together, but we weren't really friends – we barely knew each other and there was no trust between us. I trusted no one.

I was right not to trust them. A day came when our camp was attacked by the Romans. Several of our 'friends' were 'missing' and they were in fact the ones who had told the Romans of our lair. I dare say it was done for a reward, and I dare say had I known a reward was offered, I might have done the same.

So followed weeks of languishing in a Roman jail, and the next time that I felt fresh air on my face was the day I was crucified."

His eyes took on a far-away look. "I remember the squalid jail and how I was treated there. I remember the treatment. I know that that last day was one of agony. But it's strange – I can't recall the sensation of pain. I know I was in terrible pain, but I can't remember how it felt."

The listening women nodded. They understood. They were in the celestial city. There was a constant joy that throbbed in the air here and filled the heart with gladness. They too could remember times when, back on earth, they had wept with grief. But even the word 'grief' meant nothing here. Sadness had been destroyed by this overwhelming joy. It was just a memory of a feeling. He continued his story,

"Like countless prisoners before me, I screamed and fought them. Even as they hung me on that cross. There was another. A robber like me. He too screamed at them, making the air foul with his curses. Even so, deep down, despite my protestations, I knew I was getting what I deserved, and I suspect the same was true for him. But anger was our only defence as we hung there, helpless and naked.

My mind, my heart, my spirit were half dead already, but my body refused to give up just yet. I hoped the end would be swift and painless, but knew it wouldn't be.

We would hang there in torment. Bleeding. Slowly suffocating. Cursing this world and everything in it.

That was where I met him. Face to face. In that field. On that grassy hill. On a cross. They were crucifying him too, but his was like no crucifixion I had ever seen. He was in a worse state than us – he had been brutally tortured and his body was broken even before they had nailed him to the cross. But he didn't fight it. He didn't protest his innocence – yet even I knew enough to know he had committed no crime.

They left us alone to our agonies – but not him. They continued to taunt and mock him even after the cross jolted down into position – a movement that ripped apart more muscles, flesh, and joints, and brought excruciating spasms. He cried for water, but no one gave it. They did offer him the myrrh that would have dulled a little of the agony, but to my amazement he turned his head away. Did he want to feel the pain? There was a sign over his head proclaiming, 'King of the Jews', and this only fuelled the mockery. The soldiers and onlookers taunted him. "If you are the king, save yourself!" He made no reply.

On the third cross, my fellow prisoner joined in the mockery, directing his anger now at this man who chose to suffer in silence. I started to join in as well, but the words felt strange on my tongue. He didn't react in any way. He just hung his head and took our insults. I saw his pain wracked gaze sweep across the crowd, and then stop as they rested on his weeping mother.

"Dear woman, here is your son." He gasped the words, and for a moment I thought he was referring to himself. He continued, however.

"Here is your mother." Then I noticed one of his friends who had been standing nearby. The man moved over to the woman and held her. This Jesus was arranging the care of his mother from his cross! And his voice as he spoke the words! Yes, it was a broken instrument, full of pain, but there was such love in his voice. How could anyone feel love while they were being killed in this most brutal and shameful way?

His next words undid me. They were spoken softly - almost in a broken whisper but, strangely, everyone there heard them. "Father, forgive them, for they don't know what they are doing."

There was a second of silence before more jeering began, but this time I didn't join in. Around my pounding head the words rang. As before, they were words spoken with love, with no sense of anger. Somehow I knew they were spoken to God. How could he ask God to forgive these Roman invaders, these brutal monsters who cared for nothing other than inflicting the most pain on him that their twisted, evil souls could come up with?

The man on the third cross was incensed. "Forgive!?" he screeched, his voice cracking. He started to curse Jesus, the Romans, and all the people watching. He railed against the injustice of it all. The depth of his desperate pain was expressed through his harsh, croaking voice.

Jesus simply continued in his silent gaze, and I could almost sense his forgiveness even of this man. His mercy struck me to the heart. All three of us were in terrible distress, but Jesus was the only one that didn't deserve it. To hear him cursed was now more than I could bear.

It took an effort to speak, but I gasped out the words to him. Ignoring more jeers from the crowd, I called over, "Don't you fear God, even as we die? We deserve to die for our crimes, but this man hasn't done anything wrong." Before my courage failed, I continued in a whisper to Jesus. "Remember me when you come into your kingdom." There may have been tears mixed with the blood on my face now – it was a long time since I had last cried. It was a long time since I had done anything for anyone else, but now, as I felt my strength seeping away, it suddenly seemed a good time to reach out and stick up for goodness. I knew that goodness – utter goodness – hung on a cross next to me. I didn't understand why, but I knew it was true. I knew that even the title over his head, intended to mock him, proclaimed the truth for all to see. It was even written in several languages. Everyone with eyes to see could know that this man was indeed a king. Who else could act with such nobility and love, even while they were naked and bleeding as they died?

I expected no reply. He seemed weaker than either of us. He was fading fast. He seemed to have become oblivious to all around him as if he was battling against mightier and more evil forces elsewhere. Even the world seemed to agree, for the skies grew dark even though it was only noon. But he spoke to me again. "I assure you," he said, again with a voice full of both pain and love, "today you will be with me in paradise."

'With me in paradise!' The words penetrated my mind until they became a mantra. Where bitter fury at my lot, at the injustice of my life – and death – had filled my mind with seething complaints, now these things were ousted and replaced by those four words of hope. 'With me in paradise.' They did not remove the pain, but they gave me hope. I repeated them silently in my head, over and over. Occasionally a stray thought arose that to believe such a thing was ridiculous. But then I would painfully turn my head towards him. I could almost feel the love flowing from his broken body, even though his head hung down and flies buzzed around him. The words of love and forgiveness he had uttered seemed to hang in the air. An irrational certainty - that I would be with him that day in paradise - rose up anew within me, quelling any doubts.

I watched him whenever I could bear to. Just having him next to me, lost as he was in some deeper fight, was a comfort beyond belief. They say that crucifixion is one of the loneliest deaths. It's so shameful to hang, naked, bleeding, unable even to refrain from soiling yourself. Utterly disgusting and repellent to both friends and enemies. A death without dignity. Every shred of pain visible and expressed. There is nowhere to hide. In spite of this, you fear death even as you crave it.

Few of those who love you can bear to watch such a thing. Yet his mother and his closest friends stayed. There no was no disgust on their faces. Simply untold grief. And heart wrenching love.

None who knew me were there. My family had long since disowned me. As for the band of robbers, even were they friends, nothing would bring them here. For in my brutal end they would see possibilities of their own destiny. Yet now I knew that I hung alongside one who loved me more than any friend. When spasms of pain washed over me I turned towards him, knowing that he not only felt the same, and worse, but that he was forgiving those who had caused it. Somehow this whole thing for him was some mighty expression of love, forgiveness and grace. Gradually it dawned on me that of all the people in the world, I was the one chosen to be closest to him in his deepest trial. Not only did I have the closest place to view such love personified but, even as he died, I was dying alongside him. No one who was ever crucified before or since could have felt, as I did by then, that it was a privilege to die in such a manner.

It was my privilege even to pray for him as his terrible cry cut into the darkness, "My God, my God, why have you forsaken me?" The agony in that scream went far beyond physical pain, even though his body had now become racked with deep spasms. The darkness seemed to grow thicker and all I could do was to hang on to those words of hope: "Today you will be with me in paradise."

Time lost its meaning. We seemed to have been hanging there forever. Every minute stretched into an eternity of unrelenting agony. The hot air seared my lungs yet I could not get enough of it as, time after time, I raised myself up by straightening my legs and putting my weight on the footrest, just in order to gain an extra deep breath. It hurt to do so, but the deep desire to cling to life overrode every objection that torn muscles and stretched tendons could raise. The body was fighting to live, though its death was sealed. But even in my agony I knew it was worse for him. His back had been torn to shreds by the cruel Roman whips, his head had been deeply pieced by the thorny 'crown', his face had been beaten and spat upon – his whole body was cut, bruised and beaten to a pulp. For him the agony had to be far, far worse than anything I felt, and yet still he was thinking of others, still he was forgiving. Still his love was poured out, even as he felt the utter abandonment of being forsaken by the God he had referred to as his Father.

Then, at some point much later, came his final whisper, "Father into your hands I commend my spirit". Something in me was relieved to hear him still call this God who had abandoned him, 'Father'. But before I could think about what that might mean, his body shifted one last time as he raised himself with his poor beaten legs to gasp one last breath. It was enough to fuel that earth shaking cry, "It is finished!" and then he slumped back down and was still. Perhaps there was relief and resignation or surrender in that cry, but strangely there was triumph in it too, as if something important had at last been accomplished. It was a powerful cry, and even the earth seemed to shake. I thought I was imagining that at first, but then I was aware that even the Romans were looking in fear at the trembling earth beneath their feet. Even they, who inflicted these punishments with cruel regularity, had never seen a man die like that before.

Now I was alone. The other robber had sunk into his own moaning, pain racked delirium. I was drifting now, semi-conscious. The Romans and other spectators seemed far away. Much nearer seemed the one who had gone. I knew he was waiting for me. I was alone now, but his words remained. "Today you will be with me in paradise."

I believed it. Even though I still thought we would be hanging for a day or two yet. But I had forgotten that they wanted us dead before the Passover. That same day they broke our legs to make sure we could not move to ease our breathing. It was a final, numbing, brutal blow, followed by shocks of tearing pain as my body couldn't stop itself from trying to move. Struggling to get that last breath which never came. The end was swift then. His words were fulfilled. In a fraction of a second I was transported from that world of dark agony to this place."

200

He grew silent. They all sat silently together, surrounded by, united by, and contemplating the love that had drawn each of them here. Even as the man had spoken so graphically of his pain, none of them, not even he, could really feel it now. His eyes had shone as he spoke, not in remembrance of pain, but in recollection of love.

"We all met him," said Lydia at last — and it could have been moments or hours later - "on a field. On a hill. How freely he gave himself. How completely. How utterly and individually he loves each one."

They considered the vastness of heaven and the numbers of souls there, knowing that somehow He knew and loved every one of them individually. They were each of them different, and yet each of them was one now, with him.

Miriam stood and the others followed.

"Let's go to the throne. Let's worship."

The throne, too, was on a hill, in a field. Crowned with an emerald rainbow. Myriads of angels surrounding it, on the ground and in the air. Harmonies of throbbing worship. And in the middle, the Servant King, the Lamb of God, the Lion of Judah. Praise to His wonderful name, forevermore.

• •

Meditation

Consider the mercy of Jesus. Dying not only for his friends, but for his enemies, and saving them too as soon as they turned to him.

201

So often I am unforgiving or unmerciful. Pray with me that God will soften our hearts.

Love is bleeding

Love is bleeding
Costly love
Wounded love
A gift of love
from your hands.

Your hands
stretched out and willingly offered
As cruel nails tore you
your inner gaze was fixed
on the joy set before you.

Joy? What joy?
Did our faces pass across Your vision
one by beloved one?
Was that your joy?
As eternity beckoned –
eternity shared with Father and Spirit
and now with us.

Let love's costly blood
drip down upon me.

May I stretch out my hands
and willingly offer them.
May they start to look like yours -
and should I bleed
then 'tis but an echo of your great pain

and worship
will pour from my heart

The Crucifixion

All of the angels were there. Every single one. The throbbing, love-filled community of heaven was emptied as they watched.

Some of them - even the one called Laughter - had tears flowing down their cheeks. It was the only day that Deliverance was unable to do his job. Likewise Rescue. They were under strict orders not to intervene, and they were always obedient to the Lord of Lord's commands.

They could see the Beloved suffering, but they stood back. In enforced helplessness.

Knowing why did not make it any easier. Since time began they had seen the dark stain of selfishness and sin spread across every nation, bringing sickness, destruction and death. Such a stain had to be cleaned. Only a blood sacrifice could do it. The angels had watched God's chosen people sacrificing their lambs, cattle, and even doves by the thousand. The sacrifices brought a degree of cleansing to the outside of men but, before long, the evil buried in men's hearts would rise up again. A better, purer sacrifice was needed. Something that could go deep into the hearts of men and purify them from the inside out.

The Beloved hung there, his body torn and broken. Pain too agonising to imagine. Just think of the worst pain you've ever known, and multiply it again, and again, and again....

It had begun in mockery as the soldiers had draped him in a scarlet robe and given him a staff. It led to violence as they beat him savagely with that same staff. Public humiliation followed as he dragged the rough wooden cross through the streets on his broken back. All they left him was his crown – the one that had long, mean thorns that ripped into his skull. Then came the nails. Crucifixion.

But the physical torment was simply the backdrop for the battle that raged in his mind and his heart.
He was tormented with questions and lies.

Do those things ever go around your mind? Am I worth anything? Am I loved? Am I a child of God? Does he love me? He can't – can he? Surely one who loved me would never leave me in this state?

Jesus hung there. The soldiers' spit mingled with his blood, telling him he was hated. They mocked his very being – he who was saviour, taunted with: "Save yourself!" He who was Heaven's darling was told to: "Come down from the cross, if you are the Son of God".

Soon others joined in – even the two thieves crucified with him poured out their abuse. The crowds threw his promises back at him in their blind ignorance. "You were going to destroy the temple and rebuild it in three days…"? Not realising that this was exactly what was happening before their eyes.

Then those who claimed to worship his very Father came along. The churchy lot. "Come down from the cross and we will believe you." "He trusts in God – let God rescue him now **if He wants him**…" The unkindest cut came right there from the church chiefs.

Do you hear the lies….? 'Are you the Son of God?'… 'Are you saviour?' 'Are you king?' 'Does God even want you?' His friends had long since fled. The thorns dug in, like burning needles.

The angels were silent.

They had seen it all. Some were those who had visited the shepherds on the night of his birth, trumpeting out the joyous news.

Others had comforted him after those forty long days in the desert.

The angels had always shone like the sun. Now, however, they took out black robes which they had never worn before, and never would again. Silently, at the sixth hour, they donned them. Now the sky turned black. For three long hours a dreadful hush fell.

Now was the darkest hour, when all would be won or lost. The Beloved was alone in the blackness. None could see his agony now.

This was the moment when he allowed the dark sin of mankind to fall on him. And the lies blended strangely with the truth, for now his Father had indeed turned away. His glory was unable to look upon the sin and Jesus became somehow unwanted by his Father. Abandoned.

His agonised cry, "Eloi, Eloi, lama sabachthani..." still echoes around the world whenever the consequences of sin's destructive force erupts in fire, earthquake or famine - "My God, My God, why have you forsaken me?"

He fought alone. No angel helped. Even the Father had turned away – His heart even more torn and broken than the body that hung on the cross. Who knows the mystery of how Jesus conquered, but finally the triumphant cry of, "It is finished!" tore the darkness. A final whisper: "Father, into your hands, I commit my spirit," left no doubt that his heart had withstood the onslaught.

As his spirit fled the earth, as one the angels threw off the black robes for Jesus to take and burn in the depths of hell, never to be seen again. Some flew to the so-called temple and ripped the cloth that restricted the Father's presence to the chosen few from top to bottom. Many came to the earth, until the very ground shook as they landed. They landed in the burial grounds and welcomed the risen ones back, ushering them towards the city. The angels who were to be at the tomb in three days time were preparing their shining garments in delight. The enemy was in confusion - not yet understanding that his lies would never again hold the same power. For his lies had been broken.

The sacrifice was paid. The purest blood ever to walk the earth had been shed to cleanse men from the inside out.

Heaven's gates flung wide to welcome a victorious Jesus, and with him the penitent thief who had hung by his side.

A new celestial community had been birthed. One which will include all of his friends.

●●●

Meditation

In his darkest moments, and racked with pain, the heart and identity of Jesus were under ferocious attack by his enemy. Do you ever doubt that you are a beloved child of God? Why not go though the New Testament, collecting scriptures that declare this truth? Store them up, and go through them in your times of doubt. Be warned – the enemy will strike when you are at your most vulnerable – when you are in pain, or alone, or in the night. Be ready with God's truth buried in your heart.

Because you are sons, God has sent forth the Spirit of His Son into our hearts, crying, "Abba! Father!" Therefore you are no longer a slave, but a son; and if a son, then an heir through God. (Galatians 4:1-7)

The Passion

Your grace
is in your blood stained face.
Eyes full of love, oozing out kindness -
though we didn't see, such was our blindness.

Ever ready to greet, to go out and meet
were your ever moving, nailed down feet.

Your hands that touched and healed and hugged
torn to shreds by the cross you lugged.

Arms that held now stretched out wide
embraced the world even as you died.

Your beaten back took our burden and strain
though we are the ones who caused your pain.

Your heart - God's heart, once so full of love
is broken, spilt out, while the Father above
with sadness and tears streaming down His face
whispers, "Son, it is worth it for the human race."

The tomb stands empty, your power released
whilst all through your torture your love never ceased.
As we poured out our hatred, forgiveness you gave
taking our punishment, our death to the grave.

You took all our darkness, you turned it to light.
You take all our blindness as you give us new sight.

Such joy, resurrection, new life now is mine
as your cry, "It is finished" echoes through time.

Dinah's story: On The Beach

I pulled the threadbare shawl closer around my thin shoulders, shivering as I emerged from the trees. It was terribly early to be out. Thankfully the moon was almost full, for there was not yet the slightest hint of dawn. Even so, I had stubbed my bare feet several times on stones in the roads as I moved swiftly through the village. I had been praying fiercely that I would not meet anyone – either anyone dangerous or anyone who knew me. I would cop it at home if my parents knew I was out of bed at such an hour.

Long ago I had learnt the art of moving in cat-like silence. As usual I had slept in my coarse shift, though tonight it had hurt my sore back. I had risen silently from my alcove and crept past my sleeping brothers. Three of them still lived at home, though I doubted that Simeon would be around much longer now that he was working in the fields on the edge of the village. Luckily my father had built a tiny room off the back of our house - where he slept with my mother. Before he had built it my parents used to sleep in the kitchen, and I wouldn't have been able to pass through to the outside without disturbing them. The arrival of my younger brothers meant that the space had to be increased. My father had repeatedly cursed the fact that I was female. All my siblings were brothers and it would have been easier if I was a boy. I could also have earned more money. My mother grunted in agreement whenever my father grumbled about it, but secretly she was thankful that there was someone in the house to share the woman's work. I was good at sewing, too, which proved useful when it came to helping to mend the fishermen's nets. I could earn a few extra coins doing that.

I didn't mind mending nets. I actively enjoyed it. It freed me from the house in the mornings when father would kick anything that got under his feet, be it the scruffy dog that sometimes visited, or one of his children. I could be away from mother's heavy sighs and the endless demands of my brothers. The young ones were old enough now to take care of themselves – as I had been at their age – but they had now started to copy father and began ordering me around imperiously. Simeon, as a major wage earner, would not lift a finger to help anyone. So it was with huge relief that I would leave at dawn and go to the lake to see if there were any nets to mend, or even fish to clean. I really didn't mind what I did. Anything that would keep me away from the house was fine. Sometimes I would be out for most of the morning. The days when I couldn't pick up any work, I would walk home as slowly as I dared, with a heavy heart, knowing there would be little freedom from the chores for the rest of the day.

I liked it by the lake. I liked the strong smells of the fish, the feel of their slimy scales – the way they glistened in the sunlight. Even the precision needed to fix nets brought me satisfaction. Above all, I loved the sight of the vast Sea of Galilee stretching away so far that you could not see the banks on the other side. I would have loved to have gone out with the fishermen, too, but that of course was impossible. A few of them scared me, but on the whole I didn't mind their loud, brash ways. They were rough, but then so was father and, unlike him, they didn't seem to be unkind.

I was especially drawn to the lake, now that the others were back. I had thought I would never see them again. Before they went, when they still worked on the lake, Simon - the loudest of them all - had often ruffled my hair as he passed, and his brother, Andrew, was positively kind to me. He liked children, and would slip a few fish into my hands now and then. They would always let me help the other women mend their nets. But then they left. They were gone for three long years. Not from the town altogether, but they no longer fished. Now they went around with the Jewish Rabbi – Jesus - the carpenter turned preacher.

211

My father had been disgusted with them, especially when the free fish stopped coming home with me. "Thought he had more sense than that. His father's having to hire men now. What happened to respect for one's family? How's he going to look after that mother of his now? Pah! Religion!" He spat the word out, even though he went to the synagogue every Sabbath. "It causes trouble."

If the rumours were right, it possibly did cause trouble. Jesus stirred up interest wherever he went. Crowds started to follow him. I was eight at the time, and simply believed my father. It meant less fish for us, less money, and more strangers in the town. But then Jesus would go away with his new found disciples, on trips to Judea, sometimes just to villages around the lake, sometimes as far away as Jerusalem. They would be gone days, weeks, or on occasions even longer. Sometimes they would remain in the village, but I was under strict orders to go nowhere near them. I obeyed. I knew that disobedience resulted in bruises. I was cross that Jesus had taken away my fishermen (as I had thought of them) and I was a little afraid of a man who could wield such influence over strong-minded men like Simon and his friends.

Then came the day it had all changed. Two years ago, my aunt and uncle, along with their daughter, Ruth, had passed through on the way to Jerusalem. They were going to one of the big feasts there and had decided that Ruth should come too and see the big city for herself. My aunt would say, "Every child should see it once. Before long they'll be grown and married, and then they'll be tied to their home by their apron straps."

My mother had snorted in reply, "No child of mine will see the place, that's for sure!"

To my surprise, however, my aunt had replied, "But Marion, we could take Dinah with us, this very year. Ruth could do with a companion her own age. If you think she could walk the distance, that is?" She looked doubtfully at my scrawny figure.

To my amazement, my mother tilted her head on one side and thought about the idea as she considered me. She was never tender with me. She barely had time for me, except to order me around. No one, therefore, was more surprised than I when she said, "She's a good girl. Perhaps she <u>should</u> have a treat. It will probably be her first and last one. I'll speak to her father tonight."

My hope died. He would never agree to me having a treat. What I had forgotten was that my aunt was his older sister and could still wield some influence over him. She was also like a dog with a bone when an idea got into her head and, before I knew it, I was trotting alongside them, trying to keep up as we headed south. Ruth chattered non-stop. She was a year older than me and much taller. I was a little in awe of her. I hung on her every word. On that trip I saw more people than I knew existed, and many sights that astonished me. The one thing I had never expected, though, was to hear so much about Jesus. His name was on everybody's lips. The further south we travelled, the more we heard. As we reached Judea, we learned he was nearby. My aunt and uncle were not as dismissive of him as my parents. In fact, they plied me with questions after hearing me mention that once I had worked for his friends. I could, however, tell them nothing.

They were very curious about him. As we neared Jerusalem we heard that Jesus was nearby, and they seized the opportunity to try to see him. It was only a mile or two out of our way. They joined the crowds and listened to his words, whilst I played with Ruth and some other children who were there. All sorts of people were there. Even a posh child called Lydia joined us in our games. It was, in fact, Lydia's idea to push through the crowds in order to glimpse Jesus. We all followed, though we wouldn't have dared to suggest such a thing. We thought Jesus' friends would block our way once we got near. They tried to. Simon looked so stern I was

213

frightened, but Jesus cut through their objections. He insisted that we come, one by one, to be blessed. I was trembling as I approached Jesus. Unlike Lydia, who looked composed and lovely (even though she had torn her posh dress by now), I was dirty, poorly dressed, and I'm sure I must have smelt. Nonetheless, Jesus took me in his arms as gently as if I were made of china and might break.

"Why, I know you!" said a voice. I tore my eyes away from Jesus for a second and saw it was Andrew. "You're from home," he cried out. "Dinah, isn't it?"

I nodded, speechless. I was very surprised that he remembered me. Jesus' brown eyes were warm and interested. "So you know the fishermen, do you?" I nodded. "They follow me now." I nodded again and he cocked his head on one side and said, with a twinkle in his eye, "I wonder, if you were a little older, and I said, 'Come, follow me,' whether you would do so?"

I stared for a moment and then – heaven alone knows what possessed me – I threw my arms around his neck and hugged him tightly. His arms wrapped themselves around me, and I was engulfed in his cloak so that his burst of joyful laughter was muffled in my ears. It wasn't for long, but I've never felt that loved and safe, either before or since. Eventually Jesus put me down. As he did so, he cupped my chin in his hand, whispered a blessing over me that I barely heard, looked into my eyes and smiled. "Till we meet again," he had said.

The rest of the trip to Jerusalem, and then home, passed in a blur. I could think of nothing but how that encounter with Jesus had made me feel. Just thinking about him made me feel warm inside, and a shiver of joy would pass through my heart when I remembered his laugh.

That was two years ago. Now I was eleven. I never doubted I would see him again. Not after his words which I carried close to my heart. Now I would dare to disobey my father when Jesus visited. But to my frustration there was never the chance. He grew more popular. I could never get close, and the amount he travelled increased. He and his friends were rarely in the village now.

It was with horrified disbelief that I heard the first rumours.

He couldn't be dead? Not dead. Not murdered. Not crucified and tortured. Even a child my age knew what that meant. The arm of Rome was long, reaching even to this backwater.

There must be some sort of a mistake. I knew I would see him again. He had said so. I refused to believe it. I knew how rumours grew, and in the growing became increasingly twisted – until eventually there was no truth in them.

But then the fishermen returned. Not only to the village, but to their boats. When I heard the news I was at the beach before dawn, straining to make out the boats. Sure enough, there was Simon - Peter - as some called him now. One penetrating look at his face told me the truth. I saw a terrible sadness there. Other things, too, that I couldn't fathom – I was just a child – but I sensed he was a totally different man. A man who had seen things the stuff of dreams were made of - or perhaps nightmares, too.

I didn't wait. I couldn't bear to ask, to hear him speak of it. I turned away, walking blindly along the stony beach with tears streaming down my face. I was oblivious to the bare stones that hurt my feet. The pain on the inside was far greater. I was gone most of the day. That earned me a thrashing that evening from my father, to which I submitted without a murmur. I didn't care. The light had gone out of my world. I had been so sure we would meet again.

That night I had the dream again. Pushing through the crowds, desperate to see him. Reaching him. The wonderful embrace. His blessing warming me from the inside out. His look of love. His words, "Till we meet again."

I woke with a start, sitting bolt upright. I gasped at the pain in my lower back. Perhaps that thrashing had hurt, after all. My father's aim was bad. What had woken me? I listened intently but heard nothing. I remembered the dream and also the fact of his death all at once, and hugged myself in anguish. I couldn't bear to be in the house a second longer. Quietly I arose and tip-toed my way out. Into the streets. Towards the beach, knowing it would be deserted at this hour. The fishing fleet would not be back before dawn. I was praying I would meet no one – either anyone dangerous or anyone I knew. The last thing I needed was another beating.

But I had seen no one. Now I emerged onto the beach and I smiled at the moonlight sparkling on the water. It was beautiful and peaceful. The stones - which could burn on a summer's day - were now cool under my feet. It was not quite high tide and I could still see sand by the water's edge, so I made my way over to it and stood, staring out across the lake.

I don't know how long I stood there. Moments? Minutes? Longer?

Suddenly I knew I was no longer alone. I spun around, ready to run. Someone was approaching. He walked straight towards me. I was paralysed with fright, all the more so when I realised who it was. Was it a ghost? I literally shook with terror.

He stretched out his arms as he appeared. The moonlight seemed even brighter here by the water, and I stared in disbelief. I could see terrible scars on the hands that he stretched out towards me. I took a step back, not noticing that I had stepped into the sea.

216

Then he spoke, and his voice carried the same gentle warmth that it had in my memories and dreams.

"Peace. Don't be afraid. I am no ghost."

Still I stared, still full of fear. He smiled, and added with a low chuckle, "If you retreat much more, you'll get very wet."

I had stepped back again. I was still short for my age. I was knee deep.

I couldn't tear my eyes away from him. At last I whispered, my voice barely a croak,
"Is it really you?"

He nodded, and there was no mistaking the wry amusement in his face. I realised I had a choice – to run away, or to go towards him. It crossed my mind that, while I knew plenty of ghost stories, none of them concerned ghosts that had a sense of humour.

His smile grew almost as if he could read my mind. "Dinah," he said, startling me all over again with the use of my name. He remembered that? After two years, and even after being dead? "Didn't I say we would meet again?"

It was him. Suddenly I was certain. I remembered his other words, "Would I have come and followed?" As I remembered, I walked back onto the shore and and took his outstretched hands – scars and all - in my little ones.

He laughed out loud, reached down, and scooped me up, swinging me round in a circle as if I were four years old. Several things happened. Firstly, I winced as he picked me up – my back was sore – but as he spun me the soreness vanished. Secondly, the fear I had felt was replaced by a burst of joy so strong it was almost impossible to bear. Thirdly, the deep chill that had filled me as I walked through the early morning melted away, leaving me feeling warm all over.

He kept swinging me around, again and again, until he started to stagger with real or feigned dizziness until we both collapsed onto the sand in a heap of hugs and laughter.

It was a long time before I could stop laughing. My back no longer hurt, but laughing this much made my sides ache. Eventually I wiped the tears of laughter from my eyes and asked, between chuckles, "How can you be alive? And what are you doing here?"

His laughter had subsided now, but he smiled and looked into my eyes. "I am the resurrection and the life. Everlasting life. And I'm here to cook breakfast for my friends." He started laughing again, but more quietly now, as he watched my expression changer from wonder to bemusement at his words.

"Breakfast??" I said in disbelief. Yet somewhere deep down the word 'friends' had registered, and I knew I was included in that. The thought made me glad. So glad.

He was so joyful. His head shook with laughter again as he nodded.

I looked around at the deserted beach and threw my arms out in a question. "Here?"

He nodded, clearly enjoying himself immensely.

"How? Who with? What with?"

He stood, brushing the sand off his robe. "Ahhh," he said mysteriously. "You will see. First, a fire to cook with. Help me to find some wood. "

He pulled me to my feet and, holding hands, we walked across the stones to the grasses on the edge of the beach. He pulled up armfuls of grass and handed them to me to hold. He scrabbled around, collecting driftwood very quickly until he had a full armload. We turned and made our way back to the edge of the stones. Once there, he re-arranged them into a fire pit, having dumped the wood nearby.

I looked at the grasses. "These won't burn."

He grinned. "Put them down. They're to sit on."

Feeling a bit silly, I put them down a little way away from the fire pit. I sat on them. Strange — they felt softer than grass. He fiddled around, arranging the wood, and I watched, suddenly feeling a little sleepy. He put his hands deeply into the wood, muttered some words and fire sprung up. It made me jump! He seemed to remove his hands very slowly, but neither they, nor his robe, seemed burned.

Nothing about this made any sense. But I didn't care. I was happy just to be there, watching him.

Maybe he had meant it about the breakfast. But he had no food. As if reading my thoughts he glanced around and picked up a stone, much larger than the other stones nearby. It was oval shaped and filled both his hands, though he lifted it easily enough.

"What do you think? Bread and fish?" He didn't seem to expect an answer, and wasn't likely to get one, for I was dumbstruck by what was going on. Had I really woken up? I pinched myself surreptitiously on the leg. Ow! I was awake, alright. Grinning, he continued, weighing the stone in his hand.

"Someone once challenged me to turn stones into bread," he said, "I seem to remember I was very hungry at the time." Suddenly he tossed the stone towards me. Instinctively I stretched out and caught it. I had allowed for its weight and nearly dropped it completely, for it was far lighter than I had anticipated. I stared at it. It was bread. I sniffed it dubiously. It smelt delicious. "Have some," he urged happily. "Plenty more where that came from." He started collecting the bigger stones and laid them near the fire. As he placed each one down, it became bread."

"Who are you?" I whispered in wonder.

He glanced around at me, still smiling. So much joy in him, it seemed to flow out of his very being. "I am the bread of life. Stick around me, you'll never hunger again. Now. Fish...."

I tore off a piece of the bread, unable to resist it any longer. Gorgeous! Jesus strode away towards the sea and plunged straight in until he was thigh deep. I heard him quietly singing and he placed his hands, palms up, into the sea. I watched, entranced.

In amazement, I saw a flash of silver as he lifted out his palm. A small fish lay in it. It had swum right into his hand. He raised it to his face and seemed to look right into its eyes. "Thank you, little one, but you are too small. Be free, and live your life." He tossed it back in, and off it went. I shook my head – I had half expected it to say goodbye!

Moments later he lifted his hands again. This time a bigger fish was in them. I stood to see more clearly, for I could see a lot of movement in the sea around him. It seemed to be iridescent and heaving. I gasped, realising that it was fish that were surrounding him. They almost seemed to be begging him to take them.

He picked out two handfuls of fish and made his way back to where I gaped, open-mouthed. His robe seemed perfectly dry. The question was only in my eyes, but he answered gently,

"They recognise me. After all, I did make them," he added, almost apologetically with a shrug. "I'm honoured that they give themselves to be eaten by me and my friends. I know a bit about sacrifice. It's true that I died. But murder would imply that I was killed against my will." He shook his head. "It is the will of my Father that none should die. But sometimes a life needs to be given, that many might be saved."

I didn't understand, but something in his words reached me. I knew that I loved him fiercely, with all of my heart.

He quickly speared the fish and put them by the fire to cook. Then he came over to me, taking my hands.

"Come, sit down. I'll cook. You're tired. Why don't you have a rest? Lie down for a while."

He glanced towards the horizon, which seemed marginally lighter now. "The fishing boats will arrive soon, bearing my friends. I need to talk with Peter over breakfast. You rest."

I did feel exhausted. Exhilarated too, but deeply tired. I yawned. "If I sleep, will you still be here when I wake?" I saw a passing regret cross his face and realised the answer was 'no'. I started to panic, reaching out. He took my hands. "I must go soon, to my Father's house. As must you go - to yours." He moved one of his hands and placed it on my head, in much the same way that he had done two years earlier, whispering a prayer. Then he touched my breastbone, where my heart was. His voice was solemn now. "You have chosen to follow. I will always be with you. I will protect and guide you, though you may not see me."

I didn't like to ask if I would ever see him again, for once more I could see in his face that it would not be so. I felt tears beginning to well up. He took my chin in his hand and looked deeply into my eyes with love, warmth and a promise. "Dinah." My tears stopped. "Till we meet again."

With all my being I wanted to stay awake, but the fire was warm and my eyes grew heavy. I was vaguely aware of shouting and splashing some time later, as the boats pulled in, but sleep had taken me.

It was perhaps not much more than an hour later when I awoke. The fire still glowed, but no one was there now. Fish bones were strewn around, the only evidence of the feast.

Slowly I rose and stretched. I braced myself for the pain that this would cause, but there was none. I remembered – of course - he had healed my back. I thought about his words. He would always be with me. He would protect me. He would guide me.

I walked across the beach to the trees and the lane to the village. I passed the huts where the women were already at work cleaning fish. I heard a cry.

"Dinah! Wait!"

I turned. It was Andrew. He thrust a massive cloth package into my hands.

"What?-"

He smiled. "Jesus wanted you to have it. He was very insistent."

I could feel the movement of slimy fish in there. But there was something more solid than fish there. I peeked. Two large round

222

loaves of fresh bread. "Ah," I said, with excited understanding. Perhaps he really would protect me. "Stones for breakfast!"

Andrew looked puzzled, but accepted my thanks and watched me go.

My parents were up and dressed when I got home. Father looked cross initially, but his anger turned to surprise when I unwrapped the package on the table before him.

"Breakfast," I said. Something had changed. I felt no more fear for this man, my father. I almost felt sorry for him. "I'll bring fish when I can." I paused, and added - with a strange authority, part of me wondering how I dared say it even as I spoke - "But there will be no more beatings. No more cruelty."

My mother stared and cast a frightened look at my father. He, however, simply turned the bread over in his hand and glanced at me not with anger, but almost with fear. Something had changed. He gave a single nod and tore off a piece of bread.

He never hit me again.

He still lives there, though ten years have passed. But I do not. My husband, David, is a fisherman. He was there that day. He saw Andrew put the bread and fish into my arms. Andrew and my fishermen (I always still call them that, though Peter is now growing in fame as a church leader) did not linger, but moved down to Jerusalem. David told me later that Andrew had suggested I might like fish or bread now and then, but he says that even if Andrew had never said a word, something about me made him want to put fish and bread into my hands. He kept a few fish back for me, thrice a week at first, but soon daily. Love grew between us. As soon as I was old enough, we wed. I was glad to leave home. My father avoided me, for which I was grateful, and my mother seemed to soften a little towards me. It was, however, never a happy house.

Our own house is full of joy. My two children love the beaches and play there often. They love the stories I tell them of the fish who loved Jesus and wanted him to eat them. They play at turning stones into bread, but never manage it. I take their chubby chins in my hand and look with love into their eyes, and say, "If you follow him, one day you will meet him."

I hope and pray that they will. I know I will.

Sometimes at dawn I rise and stand at the water's edge, waiting for my husband to sail home.

Sometimes, if I stare at the water hard, I see a flash of silver as a fish passes.

Sometimes, if I listen hard, I believe I hear His song on the wind.

■ ■

Meditation

My imagination took the story of Jesus cooking breakfast on the beach for his friends, and embellished it. Of course, Jesus may well have brought the loaves and fish with him to cook, but I wonder... Dinah's story is, of course, of my own making, but there must be many people whose paths crossed the path of Jesus and who were never the same again.

As John says, "Jesus also did many other things. If they were all written down, I suppose the whole world could not contain the books that would be written."

As a final meditation, imagine you meet Jesus in a place of your choosing. It may be on a beach, in a wood, up a mountain or on a train. What would you say to him? Would you have questions? Ask the Spirit to show you how he would answer. Above all, look deeply into his eyes of love.

Fish!

Fish!
It was always fish with Him!
A fishing village.
Fishermen friends.
Fish to feed five thousand.

That morning the risen Christ appeared
I don't remember who suggested
we should count the fish.
Or exactly when it happened - or why?
Detail was lost in the
confused joy
of that morning.
The Morning Star
was in our midst
and transformed our aching hearts
banishing our weariness
with renewed hope.
He lit the cold darkness
with His fire
with His love.
The empty nets now straining
and bulging with fish.

Peter – beside himself –
In and out of the water like an overgrown puppy.
Dripping water and joy all over the fish
as we tried to count the slithering things.
scales on our hands
but no scales on our eyes now
We knew He was Messiah.

Peter – casting glances
now and then
226

at the man he had betrayed
just checking He was still there,
not yet able to meet His eyes
just checking it really was Him.

Jesus waited patiently
as laughing wildly
we reached 'a hundred'
Fish leapt and gasped and flopped in their death throes.
We numbered them
even as our fishing days now were numbered.

The burning coals glowed
waiting to purify.
The bread that was broken
whole again – waiting to feed.

Still he feeds us
producing riches from barren dark oceans
Still He is our bread
in all our brokenness
Still the burning coals purify.

But oh, what joy –
ridiculous laugher – that morning!
And this morning
to know He still waits
upon the shore
for our efforts to cease.
Still He invites us
to have breakfast with Him.

There were exactly
one hundred
and fifty three
fish!

References

1. The Birth

   Poem – The Birth

   Luke2: 28-15,
   Philippians 2:6-8,
   Hebrews 12:2
   Revelation 12:1-10

2. Dorcas

   Poem – Water into Wine

   Luke 4:38, Matthew
   10:42 and 26:35-45
   John 2:1-12

2. Whilst you were sleeping
   Poem – Water at the Well

   Luke 8: 22-25
   John 4:5-30

3. From Despair to Deliverance
   Poem – Had Jesus not come

   Luke 8:40-55

4. Lydia – Encounter with Jesus Part 1
   Poem – Peter's Song

   Matthew 19:13-15
   Matthew 14:22-31

5. Martha Part 1: Martha
   Poem – Senses

   Luke 10:38-42
   Mark 7:31-37

6. John: The Lord's Prayer

   Poem – Quiet time?

   Mathew 6:9-13, Luke
   11: 2-4
   Hebrews 5:7

7. Miriam – Encounter with Jesus Part 2

   Poem – Bread

   John 6:1-14, John
   6:32-35, Matt 6:11

8. The Tenth Leper

   Poem – Forgiven

   Luke 17:11-19, John
   8:1-11,Rev 21:5

9. Zacchaeus   *Luke 19:1-10*
    Poem – Imagine   *1 Corinthians 1:25*

10. Martha Part 2: Lazarus   *John 11:1-44*
    Poem – Freedom Fighter

11. Martha Part 3: Mary   *John 12:1-8*
    Poem – Worship

12. Lazarus: Bethany   *John 14: 16-27*
    Poem – Fear

13. Andrew: The Last Supper   *Mark 11: 15-17, John*
    13: 18-29
    Poem – Sit with Me

14. Jesus at Prayer   *John 18: 15-17, John*
    21:7-11
    Poem – Gethsemane

15. The Thief – Encounter with Jesus Part 3 *Luke:23:26-43*
    Poem – Love is Bleeding

16. The Crucifixion   *Luke 23*
    Poem – The Passion

17. Dinah: On the beach   *John 21:4 John 21:4*
    Poem – Fish   *John 21:11*

About the Author

Emma Bunday lives on the south coast of England with her husband, Jonathan, and their cat!

She has been producing short meditations and poems on postcard-sized photographs for some years. These can be both viewed and purchased from her website. She can also be contacted via the same website at www.poemcards.biz

This is her first book.

About the Cover

The cover is from a painting by Johanna Wilbraham. Johanna is both an artist and a dear friend.

A selection of her beautiful portraits can be seen on her website at www.johannawilbraham.co.uk